Working with Family Businesses

David Bork

Dennis T. Jaffe

Sam H. Lane

Leslie Dashew

Quentin G. Heisler

Working with Family Businesses

A Guide for Professionals

Jossey-Bass Publishers • San Francisco

Substantial discounts on bulk quantities of Jossey-Bass books are
available to corporations, professional associations, and other
organizations. For details and discount information, contact the
special sales department at Jossey-Bass Inc., Publishers.
(415) 433–1740; Fax (800) 605–2665.

For sales outside the United States, please contact your local
Simon & Schuster International Office.

Jossey-Bass Web address: http://www.josseybass.com

TCF Manufactured in the United States of America on Lyons Falls
Pathfinder Tradebook. This paper is acid-free and 100 percent
totally chlorine-free.

Library of Congress Cataloging-in-Publication Data

Working with family businesses : a guide for professionals / David
Bork . . . [et al.]. — 1st ed.
    p.   cm. — (The Jossey-Bass management series)
Includes bibliographical references and index.
ISBN 0-7879-0172-5 (alk. paper)
1. Family-owned business enterprises—Management—Handbooks,
manuals, etc.   2. Business consultants—Handbooks, manuals, etc.
I. Bork, David.   II. Series.
HD62.25.W67   1996
658'.045—dc20   95-36409

FIRST EDITION
HB Printing   10 9 8 7 6 5 4 3 2

The Jossey-Bass Management Series

Contents

Preface

The family business—a company in which ownership and management is or soon will be shared by two or more members of a family—is a challenge for any professional business advisor. It is a challenge whether the business is a very large public company under family control or a small mom-and-pop operation. Family businesses hire advisors to offer services in financial management, law, accounting, marketing, sales, and just good business practice. More often than not, these advisors find their jobs to be more complicated than they expected. The family may suffer from "too many cooks" who do not act in a reasonable fashion. The family may avoid or put off decisions, find it difficult to take any action at all, or behave counter to its own best interests and to principles of sound business practice.

Working with Family Businesses will guide family business advisors from every discipline in understanding and working through the complexity that characterizes all family businesses. No matter the area of expertise or the style of consulting that advisors embrace, they are likely to have to navigate across the invisible boundary between the family and its business. Sometimes this boundary is almost nonexistent.

The problems and complexities of the family business are not usually taught in business or professional schools, although in recent years that has begun to change. We believe that the special problems of a family business should not just be endured. We also believe that advisors cannot learn how to handle them simply through experience. Family businesses have problems that are the result of their unique nature, and the uniqueness of those problems must be addressed if we are to be truly helpful.

Professional advisors and their clients are both well served when advisors learn how to manage the problems that are bound to arise during work with family business members. In this book we explain the basic elements that comprise the family business system and share our own collective experience of almost a century of work with family businesses.

Is This Book for You?

This book is not written for family business owners and members. It is written for the accountants, lawyers, bankers, management consultants, insurance professionals, and financial advisors who help family businesses. Any professional advisor who has had difficulty in resolving problems in a family business or sometimes has felt frustrated or thwarted by the dynamics of a family will find valuable insights and guidance.

Thus, no matter what your profession, if you are a professional advisor you will find in the following pages a model for defining your role with a family business and getting the family to work together for better results in all areas.

The book distinguishes among three professional styles:

• *Expert Advisors*. Expert advisors practice their professional role as it was learned in professional school, offering knowledge for the family to use as they see fit.

• *Expert Advisors Informed by a Family Systems Perspective*. Even if advisors do not wish to change radically their style of working with family members, we believe that they can benefit by expanding their perspective on the family and the business and how the two relate. This broadened perspective, which we call the *family systems perspective*, can help advisors become more effective and avoid conflict or other pitfalls.

- *Process Consultants.* A process consultant helps families make their own decisions, understand their own will and direction, and organize themselves to deal with issues on their own. In other words, process consultants teach people how to do things for themselves.

From time to time expert advisors find themselves acting in some of the ways that process consultants do. When they do so, however, they may feel they lack guidelines on how to make the shift.

This book is not intended to turn experts into process consultants. Rather, it offers some of the insights and skills of process consulting to help expert advisors in their work with families and enable them to handle a wide range of issues and dilemmas that might otherwise thwart the successful completion of their assignments.

The book develops a model of integrated family and business dynamics to help you understand the complex reality of the family business. It will help you understand why and where difficulties may emerge and some of the pathways you may take to resolve them. The addition of this perspective will give all advisors additional leverage to manage their engagements successfully.

The book also presents tools and techniques that are used in process consulting. These tools are used by some highly successful family business advisors and can be adapted to our readers' present practices. We offer approaches for each of the key phases of the consultation process and suggest ways to address some of the common difficulties that emerge in family businesses.

Structure and Content

Part One helps you assess both your role and your client. Chapter One offers guidance in defining a comfortable and effective role in any client situation and identifying goals that meet the conflicting interests of multiple stakeholders. Chapter Two explains how to select a style of involvement—expert advisor, family systems-informed expert, or process consultant—and how to enter a family business system as a neutral third party. The chapter also helps you begin to collect and sort through fact, fiction, and perception and to help clients define their problems, sort through options, and predict outcomes. Chapter Three offers an introduction to the family business system concept and the stages of development of the system's three components: the business, the family, and the individuals within them. The chapter also provides conceptual tools to help you develop a family genogram, identify communication impediments, and assess family businesses in terms of their successful qualities. Chapter Four examines the family business system more closely, including the family's relationship to the business and its financial strengths and weaknesses, business strategy, structure, and management.

Part Two moves on to designing and implementing action. In Chapter Five you will learn how to develop interventions, decide which family and business members should be involved, and prioritize problems. You will learn what is involved in one very important intervention, the off-site family work session. Chapter Six is devoted to conflict: how conflict can be constructive and when and how to intervene when it becomes destructive. Establishing clear boundaries through organizational structures and policies is the subject of Chapter Seven.

Issues surrounding succession, wealth management, and estate planning are the topics of Chapters Eight, Nine, and Ten, in Part Three. And finally, Chapter Eleven offers a call to action for effective service to family business. Although you may not become directly involved in the family business's succession, wealth management, or estate planning, these issues are so important for family businesses that they affect many other business and personal issues. Whatever your area of expertise, your work is bound to be affected by the presence or the lack of planning processes in these areas. In turn, your work with a family business, no matter in which realm, will be affected.

A Resources section at the back of the book offers descriptions and access to further details on family business consulting.

August 1995   David Bork
                                                 Aspen, Colorado

                                                 Dennis T. Jaffe
                                         San Francisco, California

                                                 Sam H. Lane
                                              Fort Worth, Texas

                                                 Leslie Dashew
                                                Atlanta, Georgia

                                           Quentin G. Heisler
                                              Chicago, Illinois

*This book is dedicated to our families
and the families we serve.*

To Susan Manchee, my soul mate, partner, best friend.
—David Bork

*To my extended family, especially my mother, Rhoda; my
brother and sister, Brian and Cathy; my sons, Oren, Kai, and
Colton; and my wife and partner, Cynthia.*
—Dennis T. Jaffe

*To Carol Ann for her unfailing support and for being a
thoughtful and insightful sounding board; to Mother, Dad,
John Barry, and Patsy, for their unconditional regard and
patience; to Houston and Patrick for the enduring bond of our
evolving relationships—I've learned a lot; and to Rich and
Lance for our early work together—it laid the foundation for
much of the thinking in this book.*
—Sam H. Lane

*To the members of my extended family, who have taught me a
great deal about the joys and challenges of family and business
life and who have been great sources of inspiration and support
throughout my life. In particular, this is dedicated to Stanley
Dashew, entrepreneur, inventor, and loving father. He gave
me the values of industriousness and compassion that have
been the cornerstones of my life. And to my daughter, Baleigh
Dashew Isaacs, whose creativity and commitment demonstrate
how values cross many generations.*
—Leslie Dashew

To Susan, Sarah, Tom, and Meg.
—Quentin G. Heisler

Acknowledgments

To Michael Weinberg of the Madison Group, who first gave us the idea and the inspiration for this work.

To the Family Firm Institute, the professional group where we all met and under whose auspices we have attended many conferences. The Institute has helped us develop and nurture our ideas and has done much to define and further the field of family business development.

To the early reviewers of the various drafts of the book who helped us target our message and define our model. These include Joanie Bronfman, Lawrence E. Howes, J. Anna Looney, William T. O'Hara, Lorne Owen, J. Joseph Paul, Dale J. Seymour, John Wallace, Michael D. Weinberg, and all of our anonymous reviewers.

To our colleagues: Joseph Astrachan, for his encouragement and thoughts about organizational dynamics; Joanie Bronfman, Judy Barber, Lee Hausner, and John Levy for their pioneering work on the effects of wealth and money on personal identity; Nancy Upton of Baylor University, Mike Bourland, and Bob Kroney for their work in addressing family business concepts and estate planning; Mike Cohn, for his insights into family dynamics as they relate to family business finance; and Ann Dapice for her work on values.

To Neal Groff of the Madison Group; Bill Isaacs for his work on the dialogue process; Marie Kane, organizational consultant; Ken Kaye for his work on family business conflict; Marion McCollum; the Honorable Anthony James Mohr, Los Angeles Municipal Court judge; Joe Paul, E. J. Poza, and Bill Sauer of Susquehanna

University; Edgar Schein, of MIT's Sloan School of Management, for his defining of process consulting; Michael Schulman, Ted Simon, and Roy Kupkowski, addiction specialists; and Kathy Wiseman, for many kinds of support and inspiration.

To the Young Presidents Organization and the many local family business networks where we have presented our ideas and had important exchanges.

To our many clients, and especially the people who come to the Aspen Family Business Gathering each summer and share their struggles and challenges.

Special acknowledgments to Marjorie Hilts for her unfailing loyalty, good sense, and search for perfection in all she does for us and to Jayne Pearl for dealing with so many cooks, helping us decide what we wanted to say, and then helping us say it.

To what we gained from our decadelong working association with one another and our seamless work together.

In the end, while we acknowledge the contributions of many, only we can take responsibility for the ideas in this book.

About the Authors

David Bork is a leading pioneer in the field of family business counseling. Since 1970 he has had in-depth involvement with more than 315 families in business. He has helped them chart their way through every imaginable family business issue, including succession between generations, death of the founder, sale of the business, and wealth management. He is a proponent of the family systems approach to family business and pioneered the integration of family systems theory with sound business practice.

Bork is the author of *Family Business, Risky Business: How to Make It Work*. He is the founder of the Aspen Family Business Group, which is a resource for families in business that provides professional services, conferences, and individual coaching. It is based on Bork's research, which has found ten qualities shared by families that remain "positively connected" and successful in their business.

Dennis T. Jaffe is a founding principal of Changeworks Solutions (formerly HeartWork, Inc.), a San Francisco–based organization development firm, and professor of organizational inquiry at Saybrook Institute, San Francisco. Jaffe has worked with organizations, families, and family businesses for more than three decades. In his consulting practice he deals with succession, communication, organization development, and long-range planning. Jaffe is also a consultant to public organizations and corporations managing organizational change, developing strategic visions, and designing collaborative workplaces.

Jaffe has been deputy chair of the Research Council of Healthy Companies, a MacArthur Foundation–funded project. He earned his bachelor's degree in philosophy, his master's in management, and his doctorate in sociology, all from Yale University. His professional training is in organization development, and he is also a licensed clinical psychologist and family therapist.

Jaffe is the author of thirteen books, including *Rekindling Commitment; Organizational Vision, Values, and Mission; Empowerment: Building High-Commitment Workplaces; Working with the Ones You Love; Managing Change at Work;* and the management best-seller *Take This Job and Love It!* He has published more than one hundred professional articles. His work has been featured in publications such as the *Wall Street Journal, Nation's Business, USA Today, Business Ethics,* and *American Health.*

Sam H. Lane is a corporate psychologist who specializes as a consultant to family businesses. He is also an associate of the Aspen Family Business Group. He received his bachelor's degree from the University of Texas, Austin, and his doctorate from Texas Christian University.

During the past twelve years, Lane has helped a variety of family businesses achieve their growth goals and ensure their continued vitality. He has designed and implemented projects in succession planning, conflict resolution, strategic planning, team building, management development, organizational analysis, and development, recruitment, selection, and training. He has published articles in *Dallas–Fort Worth Business,* the *Family Firm Review,* and the *Journal of Commercial Bank Lending* and has addressed numerous professional and trade association groups.

Leslie Dashew is president of Human Side of Enterprise, an Atlanta, Georgia, organization development firm, and an associate of the Aspen Family Business Group. Dashew has combined her background in organizational development and family therapy to specialize in consultation to family businesses. She has been in practice for more than twenty years.

Dashew's work with family businesses includes prevention of serious problems by helping clients establish the policies, practices, and skills of healthy family organizations. She also works with families who are in severe conflict to help them untangle the family and business issues. Dashew is often quoted, and her writing on family business issues can be found in popular business and trade magazines, including *Nation's Business, Inc., Black Enterprise*, and *Entrepreneur*.

Dashew received her bachelor's degree in psychology from Pitzer College and her master's degree in psychiatric social work from the University of Michigan. She served on the Emory Medical School Faculty in Psychiatry for six years. She speaks widely at academic, professional, and trade association meetings and presents workshops and seminars for companies across the United States and abroad.

Quentin G. Heisler is a partner in the estate planning practice group in the Chicago office of McDermott, Will, and Emery and chairman of the firm's executive compensation group. He specializes in estate and business planning, with particular emphasis on the succession and transfer-tax problems of families that control public and private companies. He is actively engaged in the structuring of family business control and valuation devices, insurance planning to facilitate the retention of family businesses, multigenerational tax planning for wealthy families, executive compensation planning, and asset protection planning.

About the Aspen Family Business Group

The Aspen Family Business Group is an educational and consulting consortium dedicated to the development of resources for family businesses. It offers seminars for professionals, consultation to family businesses, and educational programs on various aspects of family business. Each member of the group is affiliated with a consulting or service organization in a different part of the country and is an active speaker and educator. Every summer, the group sponsors the Aspen Family Business Gathering, allowing people in family business to celebrate their success and learn from one another. The group is headquartered at 117 Aspen Airport Business Center, Suite 201, Aspen, CO 81611; phone (970) 925–8555.

Working with Family Businesses

Part One

Your Role, Your Client

In the first part of the book we present a model to help expert advisors expand and enhance their role and their perspective when working with family business problems. Family businesses present some of the same difficulties to professionals in all disciplines. In order to meet these demands, we suggest that the professional sometimes move beyond the expert role. We offer two alternative solutions when professionals are presented with situations that they cannot readily resolve through this role alone.

First, we suggest that professionals adopt what we call *a family systems perspective*, which will enable them to look at their practice from a broader context and help the family resolve some issues that may at first seem confusing or even unsolvable. Second, we suggest that professionals add what we call *process consulting skills* to their repertoire. Process consultants do not reject their own professional disciplines but take on an expanded role of teacher in order to help the family learn and grow. Many professional advisors already do many of the things that we are calling process consulting. In this book we offer a systemic introduction to some of these skills to help family business advisors become more effective.

Chapter One outlines the new role and the situations in which it may be useful. Chapter Two helps professionals establish their new role with the family, whether in an initial consultation or in a redefinition of their involvement after a long advisory relationship. A case example presents a demanding and complex family dilemma in which an advisor shifts from an expert role to a process consulting role in order to help a family business client through a crisis.

Chapter Three presents an overview of the family systems perspective. The perspective goes beyond any particular discipline in an attempt to make sense of the complex and continuously evolving relationships that exist in a family business. Chapter Four presents some of the basic elements included in an assessment of the family-business interface.

Chapter One

Advising the Family Business

There are families and there are businesses. Most people usually think of the two as independent units that operate according to completely different sets of rules. But the exception is the rule for most family businesses, both large and small. Composed of family members who share ownership and management, these companies keep the boundaries between family and business open, with the issues of the family crossing into the business and the issues of the business impinging on the family.

Into the breach step a variety of family business advisors who help families and businesses manage their financial, legal, and management affairs. These professional advisors are accountants, bankers, lawyers, financial managers, management consultants. As advisors, they have complex roles. They serve the family, the business, or both. Sometimes they cannot be sure where the family ends and the business begins.

The issues advisors face include conflicts between members of the family and conflicts between the needs of the family and the needs of the business. These conflicts arise no matter what the advisor's professional background. Such conflicts can crop up during estate planning as members fight about fairness to shareholders, in charting the future of a business, in choosing the business's next leader.

Professional advisors who work with family businesses face a dilemma: the family's actions raise issues and create conflicts that deeply affect the advisors' activity. Yet they are often unprepared or unable to handle these conflicts. Avoiding them can be disastrous;

trying to work around them can backfire. Professional advisors can be effective for many family businesses. Yet estimates from an informal poll we conducted of advisors suggest that as many as half of their cases are adversely affected by family conflicts.

This book offers professional advisors of all types a unified perspective and some concepts, tools, techniques, and guidelines for practice when family issues intrude upon professional work. Our goal is to inform advisors so that they can navigate successfully through the common conflicts and difficulties that arise in family businesses. For those who are brave and ready to experiment, we also offer some concrete techniques that can be incorporated into their practices for successful resolution of some of the more difficult situations.

The Drama of Family Business

When things go smoothly for a family business, life for both family members and employees can be wonderful. At best, a family business is free of pressures for short-term profits. It has the foresight and power to take the long view, saving, reinvesting capital, and seeing the business as a legacy for its heirs. Unlike the entrepreneurial business, which is founded on a single person's vision, the family business, when founded or led by two or more caring family members, tends to extend that caring family feeling to long-term employees. The business can be a source of pride and a livelihood for many family members who enjoy harmonious relations and meet one another's financial and personal needs.

However, a family business may also endure mediocrity, especially when owners feel an obligation to employ family members, whether or not they have the training, experience, or drive to do the job. In such cases, it can be hard for professional management teams to help or for new ideas to take root. The founder may be autocratic as well as paternalistic. The owner may have little time left for the family at home; nonworking spouses may feel lonely

or left out and resent the business. There may be a clash of interests between business and family and feelings of unfairness and
injustice.

When things do not go smoothly, life for family members and
employees alike can be a living hell. Parent is pitted against child,
sibling against sibling. Nonfamily employees and advisors can get
caught in the middle. All the while, the company may be held
hostage by the family's failure to resolve differences. Family relations deteriorate, leading to deep feelings of hurt, misunderstanding, or estrangement.

There are well-known horror stories, too: the Shoen family—the
owners of U-Haul—whose deposed president won a multimillion-
dollar lawsuit against his children, for example. There are many less
sensational but just as devastating examples of the havoc wreaked
on families in business.

However, much of the time these experiences can be avoided.
Family business advisors can usually locate a moment in the
sequence of events where there was opportunity for an intervention
that could have led to a very different outcome. The case of the
Bingham family of Louisville, Kentucky, presents an example of
such an opportunity missed. The Binghams owned a communications empire that included the Louisville *Courier Times*. In 1976,
all family members became part of the board of directors. But they
were given no business education program, which might have created a unified way of thinking about the business or a common
premise for expectations about its performance. Predictably, relationships deteriorated. Some family members on the board of directors demanded a greater say in business policies. Ultimately, both
business and family fell apart: parents were estranged from children,
the business was sold, and the patriarch died a disappointed man,
having seen the family's business empire fall apart.

Less extreme family business problems often arise when the family tries to solve problems and make decisions without the needed
tools, including structures, procedures, and learning skills. One role

of the professional advisor is to provide the problem-solving structure needed in each situation.

The overriding challenge for the family that owns and operates a business is to professionalize the manner in which all members carry out their responsibilities. To accomplish this, family business owners must develop clear goals and expectations that extend to all elements of the business, including how family members think about it. They also need to develop an employment policy that allows only competent family members to be employed.

Among the variety of advisors employed by family businesses, corporate counsels and legal advisors advise the owner. Accountants offer consulting services, prepare the corporate and individual tax returns, and do the annual audit. Management consultants create the business structure, advise management about how to deal with regulatory, tax, and operating problems, and assist owners in the final disposition of the business. Bankers become intimately involved in the business's financial affairs. Financial and estate planners help maintain and enhance the family's wealth and preserve it over generations. Insurance professionals help the family manage its risk. And a variety of other consultants may be retained to analyze specific operating problems that arise from time to time.

Each advisor has a special role in helping owners address the challenges in the constantly changing family and business. Competent advisors acquire a sound understanding of aspects of the business situation as part of their professional training. But when the client is a family business, we believe that they also need a sound working knowledge of how families interact. We have seen cases in which advisors are on firm ground about the content of their advice but not very surefooted about the best way to offer it so that the family can accept it and put it to use. This book offers professional advisors of every discipline the understanding, sensitivity, and tools they need to be effective family advisors.

Family members may look to advisors to help them manage conflicts and to make the best decisions about the future of the business. Management, shareholders, and outside directors may become comfortable with an advisor's advice and rely on it to help resolve many business or family problems, including the transition of control at the death of the principal shareholders, the succession of senior management, the sale or disposition of the business, the determination of the proper financial return for nonactive shareholders, and the termination of a nonperforming executive who also happens to be a member of the family controlling the company.

The resolution of these issues may require far more from advisors than their professional discipline has prepared them to provide. Their recommendations may be swept away in a complex wave of emotion that may not be articulated or even understood by either the advisor or the family. The family's approach to business problems may be irrational, personal, selfish, petty, acrimonious.

The family's presence looms behind many business issues. A family is a complex, multifaceted, and emotional system. Every member has different perspectives, values, needs, and abilities. The interests of every one have a place on the playing field. If not careful, an advisor can feel like a football being kicked back and forth or squashed by three-hundred-pound tackles from opposing teams. One family member may trust the advisor, another may not. The advisor may not be getting all the information needed to do the job. Simple tasks may not get done. An elegant solution based on professional expertise and offered in a rational business context may be ignored.

How, then, should an advisor proceed? When the underlying issues facing the family and its business are not properly articulated or understood, the solutions presented by the advisor may be deemed inappropriate or simply not feasible. A resolution that is clearly in the family and business interest may not be adopted. Unfortunately, the basic training of most professionals who serve families in business does not prepare them to understand interaction within families. To unlock the deepest and most lasting solution, one must understand and address the psychological issues that hold the solution captive.

Defining Your Role

This book is not intended to turn professional business advisors into psychologists. However, in order to help a family deal with matters such as estate planning, business ownership transfer, inheritance, or the future of a business, every advisor must understand the dynamics of family relationships. This book offers tools to help assess the life stage, sophistication, and health of a family, the individuals within it, and the family business. You will learn how to develop interventions to enable you to provide better advice and assistance. You will understand how to establish procedures and systems to help the family address and resolve emotional and business challenges and approach the future from a stable foundation. You will learn about new skills from which you can pick and choose.

Working with family-owned businesses is an art. There is neither a perfect solution nor a single route toward a solution to the complex circumstances presented. To serve family-owned businesses, you must learn to recognize and accept the family's stage of development and help it integrate possible solutions into its own unique personal needs and dynamics; the less than perfect or creative solution may be the one that best fits the special family situation before you.

Although the advisor may want to get things over with quickly—may wish for speedy deliberations that end with the acceptance of the advice given—family members may need time to work out their own needs and their version of an agreement. This demands patience on the advisor's part, as he or she balances a desire for expeditious resolution with the psychological realities in the family.

Different family business advisors—lawyers, accountants, bankers, financial planners, insurance professionals, management and organizational development consultants, family therapists, and so on—must resist working in isolation and secrecy. It is best when advisors work as a team with other advisors the family may have hired, pooling their knowledge and offering advice with one voice. Solutions coming from only one perspective may have important consequences for other aspects of the family business system. Open collaboration among advisors allows them to identify and address the possibilities collectively. Ideally, professionals should be able to have an open discussion about the best interests of the business. When these discussions are held in the presence of the family members involved in the business, the advisors model the ability to discuss differences and find a resolution.

The Integrated Approach to Family Business

This book synthesizes years of work and various bodies of knowledge that have helped us understand the interpersonal dynamics found in the business that is family owned and operated. We call our perspective the *integrated approach to family business* because it integrates an advisor's professional skills with an understanding of the nature of families. Recognition of the different life stages and stylistic patterns of each of the players in a family business will often explain positions taken and give insight into how to modify those positions so an amicable solution can be reached.

The integrated approach explains how disparate interests and objectives develop within a family, how stakeholders become stuck and intractable, and why they may resist rational, "professional" solutions. Because family businesses frequently include two or more generations of a family, this book addresses the significance of family traditions, expectations, and perceptions in the resolution of business issues.

The term *integrated* also refers to our belief that professional advisors can add value to their services when they blend their work with that of other advisors.

Most important, the book examines how to construct a framework to resolve business problems, manage conflict and individual differences, and identify the significant family groups. As you work your way through the book, we will assist you in positioning your-self to maintain credibility with each of the groups and outline solutions that are technically sound and accommodate the relevant interests within the family. We do not intend to help professionals become better at the mechanics of their professions. However, by adopting a broader perspective on your work, you will become more effective family counselors in the pursuit of your professions.

When it is working, the relationship between an advisor and a family business is deeply personal. Although an advisor may become very intimate with the family, the closer one gets the more one becomes aware of the issues that underly the basic premises on which the family operates. But one must be careful to maintain professional objectivity. A family business advisor who feels "almost like family" is at risk of undermining the working relationship.

Styles of Consulting and Advising

There are two main styles of professional consultation: *process consulting* and *expert advising*.

Expert Advisors

Many family business advisors only offer expert advice. They are paid to have the answers. The client and the advisor assume the goal is to find the right answer. When the advisor offers the right solution, it is assumed the family will accept and implement it. These advisors share answers but do not teach clients how to find the answers themselves.

Process Consultants

However, working with family-owned businesses often demands the skills of process consulting as well. Process consultants have special skills to address and resolve matters within the family business system. They work with the participants in the system to develop the skills they need to resolve an issue. Together with the family they inquire into the presenting dilemmas and investigate alternative solutions. When they help a family understand the dynamics of the system and create their own solutions, they alter those dynamics. The problems tend to stay solved.

The process consulting style assumes that solutions lie within the power of the group. The advisor's task is to facilitate the group's development, to develop skills within the group so it can become more autonomous in its functioning. As the saying goes, "Give a man a fish and he eats for a day. Teach a man to fish and he eats for life." The process consultant is a teacher, a guide, and a coach. Process consultants usually focus on a task or collection of tasks that, when completed, lead to an end of their relationship with the family or the creation of a new relationship.

This long-term focus may also be true of expert advisors who have durable relationships with the client as a result of special knowledge or expertise that guides the business over a long period.

Neither style of consultation is superior to the other. Sometimes the family business advisor does better by taking more time to help the family learn how to solve problems, sometimes the advisor can be most effective by simply offering an answer.

Family Systems–Informed Experts

Finally, in some cases a third role may come into play: one may be a more effective expert advisor when one understands the family dynamics that lie behind the business. We call this a *family systems–informed expert role*. Although still acting as an expert, familiarity with the broader systems issues of family business causes the advisor to ask more questions and seek information from more sources.

Chapter Two offers an exercise to help you weigh your level of comfort and skill in acting as expert advisor or process consultant for different degrees of problem resolution.

Dealing with Multiple Stakeholders

One attorney we know—we'll call him Maury Segal—represented a family business and the two older family members for years. The two trusted Maury's judgment. Their seven children, some of whom worked at the family business and all of whom owned shares, also worked with him in a more limited way. They considered him to be their advisor as well. They looked upon him as the wise family counselor and were not inclined to question or distrust his advice even when their interests seemed to be harmed by following it.

Maury Segal wore many hats in his dealings with this family. As a result, he faced some relatively complex ethical problems. Consider the multiple parties involved: the corporation, the principal family shareholders, the family officers and directors, family minority shareholders, spouses, trust entities—Maury had been involved in developing them all.

Maury avoided direct conflict because he acted as an information gatherer, facilitator, and architect for designing solutions that met the diverse stakeholders' common interest—the health of the business. Had each party retained his or her own attorney, the family would have had to retain nine lawyers to design and implement any decision! Independent counsel is critical to provide such things as prenuptial agreements or a second opinion about suggestions that an advisor like Maury presents. But we believe it was perfectly sensible and appropriate for Maury alone to serve this family's diverse members and their needs.

Maury did not have an easy job. Any advisor in this kind of position must deal with the ethical rules of conduct that are in force in the state of the practice. There does not appear to be a general prohibition of Maury's involvement in this situation. He must be satisfied that he can represent the interests of each stakeholder. If there was any question of conflict, Maury had to discuss his concerns with all of the participants and resolve concerns about whether he could represent them. If the interests of the parties begin to diverge, the advisor may have to withdraw from the matter or ask certain parties to secure outside counsel. In Chapter Seven we discuss in detail how to balance diverse stakeholder interests.

Defining the Client

A special committee of the American Bar Association (ABA) has been meeting to examine the issue of defining the client when a lawyer is serving individuals, families, and family-owned businesses. Doing so can be a confusing and conflicting matter. For example, who is the ultimate client when a professional creates a trust for a client, then serves as the professional advising the trustee, and then continues to advise the maker of the trust as well as the trust's beneficiaries? The canons of the legal profession have specified the role of the professional in these situations but years of practice have moved the issue into a gray area. Similar situations hold in other professions.

Advisors are more effective when they clearly identify their client. Should the focus be on the current owner, the future successor, or the entire family or business? Choosing one over the other may place an advisor smack in the middle of warring factions—a difficult and treacherous position for any professional.

Process consultants, including the authors of this book, often view the family business system as the client. However, expert advisors may be in a position that requires them to define the client as one individual or subsystem. For instance, an estate planner or insurance professional must first and foremost consider the interests of the individual who hired him or her. In contrast, an accountant may be bound to serve the financial needs of the business. Once the client is clearly defined, though, the advisor should not put on blinders to the surrounding systems and stakeholders. One can and should always be aware of the impact that recommendations and actions may have on the rest of the system. In this way, the advisor becomes the advocate for a strong, healthy, fiscally sound business that balances competing interests in a way that preserves the well-being of the business and the family. A balanced family business system not only produces a good return to its owners but also provides a stable, predictable place of employment for its employees, compensating them fairly on the basis of merit and industry norms. The business is usually the family's largest single asset. When the business prospers, the benefits of that prosperity accrue to the owners. But the advisor must take care to look out for the business; if the business fails or weakens, it will not meet the family's needs.

At times, the owners and other family members may take positions that are deleterious to the business. Their emotional or personal needs can move them in directions that prudence would not. When the client is defined as an individual or a subgroup of the family, there is the risk of being caught in the middle of these factions and rendered impotent in serving the interests of any of them.

But when the family business system is the client, the advisor can confront all individuals and advise all that their positions are not in the client's best interest. Thus the advisor is not the advocate for any individual but tries to look at the needs of the business and the family and help the family and the business find a balance. Defining the client in this way takes some getting used to by everyone. The client is at once broader and more ambiguous than a one-person client. Furthermore, if one person was previously the client, the advisor may have to announce the redefinition of his or her role. We will say more about this in the next chapters.

Identifying Your Goal

For some advisors, the ideal goal may be for all family members to love and respect one another and for the business to be enormously profitable. Because of the unlikelihood of reaching this goal, there must be compromises. Yet one can still accomplish a great deal and feel good about doing it. We demonstrate this concept in Figure 1.1.

Figure 1.1. Family and Business Goals.

	Family	
Hate one another	Work together	Love one another

	Business	
Go into bankruptcy	Provide a good living	Produce maximum profit

Figure 1.1 contains two continua: one represents the family, the other the business. The status of the business may range from bankruptcy to profitability. The status of the family may range from hate to love. The point on the business system continuum deemed *providing a good living* is the threshold for the minimum acceptable position in any business. A similar threshold point for the family system is *working together*. If an advisor can get the family to work together well enough to run the business and experience a minimum of acrimony and destructive conflict and if he or she can help make the business sufficiently successful to produce a good living, then that advisor has done a good job.

We believe these goals are realistic and serve all constituencies. Some degree of discontent and conflict is not only unavoidable but also inherent in a healthy, well-run business. If an advisor can help reduce conflict to acceptable (but not destructive) levels then the business can go forward. There may be times when advisors feel they are not making progress. It may help to remember where the group was when the process started and the degree to which it has moved forward.

Incremental change is evolutionary. It takes time. Many family business projects take at least two to three years. There are few quick fixes in this work. We encourage advisors to trust the process to produce the changes they seek.

A Model for Process Consulting

The tools, models, and skills that we present in this book share six underlying principles:

Work with Whole Systems

A family cannot be understood in parts or in bits. In order to solve a difficulty for one dimension of the family the advisor must begin with an inquiry into the nature of the family as a whole. The whole is understood through the lens of what we call the *systems perspective on the family business*, which we present in Chapter Three.

Balance the Needs of All Stakeholders

Almost every family business challenge presents itself as a clash between different interest groups or individuals. A lasting resolution of any issue in a family business must balance the needs of multiple groups of stakeholders. As we demonstrate in Chapter Five, the goal is to find win-win solutions.

Emphasize Communication

The path to resolution of any issue begins when all parties get together and share relevant information. Many conflicts stem from different people having incomplete information, producing different initial premises. Sharing information in a setting where people are listening rather than arguing is a big step toward resolution. We illustrate this throughout the book and especially in Chapter Six.

Develop Business Structures and Personal Boundaries

Business and emotional boundaries and business structures such as boards of directors and family councils or forums provide systematic vehicles for airing problems and procedures for resolving family business issues. We present two models for such structures and procedures in Chapter Seven.

Help the Family Business Grow and Change as Its Components Evolve

Families evolve continuously. Yesterday's solutions become today's problems. As you will learn in Chapter Three and Chapters Seven through Ten, owners must learn to grow and change together, to question the past as they focus on the future.

Find Opportunities to Collaborate with Other Professionals

Family businesses are complex systems and require a range of advice. It is rare that any individual or even professional practice offers all the perspectives a family business may need. It is important that advisors learn about other experts who can complement their perspectives and feel comfortable collaborating as part of a team.

Summary

In this chapter we set the stage for the book's discussions, in which we offer tools and perspectives to help family business advisors in any profession handle their roles. When family conflicts crop up, the advisor sometimes has to broaden his or her role and engage in new activities to be effective. Professionals must also recognize their roles. Family-owned businesses carry inherent ambiguity and potential for conflict; that will not go away. Advisors can expect to move between the roles of process consultant and expert advisor. To do this they will need constantly to address this ambiguity with the client group.

Chapter Two

Defining, Refining, and Renegotiating Your Roles

Work with any family business begins with defining your relationship and specifying the scope of the job—what will be done and what won't be done, the sorts of results that can be expected, and the potential surprises or unexpected events that may crop up. If you have an ongoing relationship as an expert advisor to the family, you may need to redefine your role for the purpose at hand. It is also important to create a trusting relationship with all the parties involved, not just the person who actually hired you, because you may need to expand your work relationship with one person to several others in the family.

This chapter examines the process of defining, refining, and renegotiating your role when you begin a problem-solving process with a family or family business. Although much professional literature deals with the *terms* of engagement, little is written about the *process* of engagement. This chapter describes the unique and delicate features of contracting and beginning work with a family business, including decisions about level of involvement. We outline skills applicable to all professional disciplines that can enhance work with a family. Establishing effective roles and expectations can diminish potential disagreements or misunderstandings about how the work with the family will be accomplished.

Choosing a Style of Involvement

We suggested earlier that advisors may benefit from developing the skills that we call *process consulting*. In many cases, an advisor's particular discipline will more than adequately get the job done. Often, though, the complexity and special nature of family businesses can make it difficult for experts in any field to serve their clients well. For example, if an advisor is hired to shore up a family's financial relationship to the business, he or she may have to wade through issues the clients prefer not to discuss, such as assumptions about individual family members' compensation. We believe that the ability to work with family businesses can be enhanced by broadening one's knowledge of family systems. The family system perspective allows advisors to identify previously unrecognized family needs and solutions.

Under which circumstances should you add some of the tools of process consulting to your expert role? Your decision to do so should be based on several factors: the degree to which the family is willing and able to discuss sensitive issues; the degree to which the identified problems have advanced; the level of conflict in the family; and your own comfort and skill in dealing with the intertwined, interpersonal dynamics and business problems.

Any decision to augment your expert role of counseling and advising to include process skills should depend on the degree of complexity and conflict in the family and its business. As Table 2.1 illustrates, the more conflict and distress a family business exhibits, the less comfortable an advisor may feel in expanding into a process consulting role even though more process skills may be required to resolve the issues. In such cases, the family systems perspective allows an advisor to identify underlying problems and recommend that the client bring in a specialist for help in those areas.

Whatever your specific area of expertise, we believe you are likely to benefit the family most if you not only give them advice but also work with them to assess and resolve the broader issues involved. However, we also maintain that crossing this line is not easy and is not necessary in every situation. We are not suggesting that advisors abandon their basic expert approach and the professional methods they have developed in order to become a family

Table 2.1. Styles of Advisor Involvement.

	1 Expert Advisor	2 Family Systems– Informed Expert	3 Process Consultant
A Prevention of problem	Offer guidelines and tools related to professional area of expertise.	Define areas for healthy growth and development; help family begin to act on them.	Help family clarify boundaries and install systems, such as board of directors and family forum.
B Rumblings of conflict or problem	Offer guidelines and tools, flag potential problems, keep a close watch.	Make clients aware of problems and their possible effects; explore ways to deal with them.	Engage family in open discussion of issues and explore possible solutions.
C Significant problem or conflict	Offer guidelines and tools along with professional suggestions for course of action.	Offer structural and procedural suggestions to help clients deal with problem themselves.	Engage family in systematic problem-solving procedures.
D Full-blown crisis in family, business, or both	Offer guidelines and tools; refer clients to specialists to work on interpersonal issues.	Set up interim structures and solutions, maybe with the help of outside experts, to gain control over the issue.	Help family deal with financial, emotional, and business problems to resolve issues and lead to renewal.

business consultant. But they can broaden their approach with an added sensitivity to the issues that are unique to family business situations.

The tools and perspectives of process consultants can be helpful to practitioners in any area. These additions to the tool kit can also help advisors avoid the pitfalls and difficulties that arise from running unknowingly into deeper family issues.

One of the first things you must determine is how comfortable, skilled, and ready you feel to move into new areas. You may be able to integrate some of the tools and perspectives presented in this book as dilemmas arise to lead you forward. For instance, you might begin by using some tools in your assessment or inquiry process and then draw on more complex techniques as you become comfortable with your new role and the new techniques.

Table 2.1 identifies appropriate styles of involvement for different clients. Across the top three styles of involvement are listed: expert advisor, family systems–informed expert, and process consultant. The left-hand column lists a continuum of problem severity. Each cell in the grid describes a style of involvement for each level of problem.

As the table shows, expert advisors limit their involvement to professional areas of expertise. Family systems–informed experts also focus primarily on the tools of their profession but do so in the context of the broader family issues that may affect the business. Process consultants add the skills needed to engage the family to work together to resolve problems and develop the internal resources to continue growing.

Each of the three types of professional involvement are valid. Most important, no role is fixed for all time. The advisor's professional approach may change with each client. The role may even change over time with the same client if circumstances warrant.

For example, suppose your client has no next-generation members in the business but your assessments reveal diverse levels of relevant business skills, motivation, and competence, as well as brewing rivalries, among the family's younger generation. The degree of problem manifestation is an A or maybe a B on Table 2.1. With your knowledge of individual stages of life (which you will learn about in Chapter Three), your response to the problem might be located in the A2 quadrant: while providing your expert services, you might point out the potential issues if younger family members were to enter the business. If you are comfortable using process consulting tools you might move into quadrant A3, helping the family install a mediating structure such as a family forum and clarifying boundaries by drafting an employment policy.

If some younger-generation members already in the business are not getting along well with one another or with their parents (the business owners) but so far have not allowed the friction to erupt into a full-blown conflict, the family business client is at the B level. An advisor who feels perfectly comfortable applying process consulting tools at the A level might be reluctant to get so involved at a more advanced problem stage. He or she may feel more comfortable offering professional services at the B2, C1, or D1 levels.

In other words, the more serious a problem, the less some advisors—regardless of their experience in their professional specialty—may feel comfortable engaging in interpersonal family dynamics. You need to find your own comfort level for each client case.

As you define the styles with which you feel most comfortable in each situation, you can explore what other resources the family might need and help the stakeholders make use of those resources. This may require doing the following:

- Recommending that the client bring in an additional advisor
- Collaborating with other advisors already working with the client
- Working proactively with other advisors as an integrated team

Clients who are in conflict sometimes try to "split" advisors, attempting to align them with their individual points of view. When several advisors work together, it is important that all are clear about their individual roles, how they will communicate with the client, and how they will communicate among themselves. It is important not to be seduced into competition for "most favored consultant" status.

There are few textbook answers in this book (or elsewhere) for working with family businesses. We offer a set of general principles that can be applied to personalize individual styles and approaches.

But advisors must be prepared to squeeze, shape, and mold their roles, strategies, and techniques to fit the family's problems and their own experience in dealing with those kinds of problems.

Interpreting Family Issues

How can you tell if a family has unresolved issues that might impede your work with them? Here are some clues:

- They don't complete their work or send you the data, such as financials, that you expect.
- The data they share don't add up, they don't understand their data, or they disagree with them.
- They send mixed messages: their words don't match their actions or emotional tone.
- They are late to meetings or postpone meetings frequently.
- The most critical family members don't show up.
- People in different parts of the family and the business say different things.

If any of these signs are present, you need to look more deeply at the family system before you can help. It is important not to ignore the signs but to understand that something deeper is going on.

Rules of Engagement

Because consulting and advising may mean different things to the family and to the advisor, it is necessary to define explicitly what will and will not be done. An effective contract—between the advisor and the business or the family—must be clear and protect the interests of both parties. For instance, an estate planner should create a contract that defines the client, the scope of the engagement, the objectives, the fee structure, and the time frame for the engagement. For example, compensation experts called in to determine compensation of two top family and three top nonfamily executives should specify that and then describe how they will do it: they will survey the marketplace and literature for similar businesses in order to recommend salaries that are in keeping with the market. As noted, the contract should also define the client, specify to whom the report will be delivered, and explain that in the course of data collection other issues that require specific attention in order to implement the estate or compensation recommendations may be identified. The advisors may also talk about how they will work with the various family stakeholders.

Advisors must set an example of clarity, expressing their values and expectations up front. Nothing should be assumed in a realm as complex as that of a family business. The advisor has to do some teaching and exploring because some of the actions he or she will take may go beyond the family's initial expectations.

In other words, the engagement rules must be flexible, enabling the advisor to adapt to unexpected events. One never knows what one may uncover as the data are collected. Perhaps the stated method of decision making in the company is light-years from the reality; for example, while the family espouses a participative process the data suggest that Mother makes all the decisions. That issue—the existing decision process—will have to be addressed in order to implement any recommendations.

The rules must also be shared, not just with one part of the family or the business but with all stakeholders who have some legitimate concern for the outcome. The task of negotiating a contract is difficult when a large family business is involved. Yet the process sets an example for how the family can work together and often is the first time they work together to resolve issues among them. We note once again that advisors' actions and behavior should serve as a model for the actions and behavior they are trying to instill in their clients.

Anatomy of a Family Business Consultation

The following case study reflects the manner in which Bruce Morgan, a skilled family business consultant, handled the issues of engagement, contracting, and entry into the family business system. It is followed by a hypothetical description of how Charlie Baker, a lawyer and family systems–informed expert, was able to use some of the same techniques to broaden his own professional focus and that of his family business client. It should be noted that Charlie Baker is a fictitious person, a composite of several advisors we know. First the account of Bruce Morgan's entry into the system.

The phone rings in my office and it is Rick. He is the son of a former client, one of three brothers who own a manufacturing business that produces heat-tolerant plastic and metal parts for the automotive industry. The company has sales of about $50 million annually and more than three hundred employees. Rick tells me there are disagreements between the three owners. He wants help resolving their differences, which he describes as "major." He has been considering activating the put that is part of their buy-sell agreement and asks me, "Do you think it is a good idea to wait or go ahead with the put?"

This situation represents a minefield of the first order. Rick has invited me to lay my professional reputation on the line before I have enough data to assess if the deal is "doable" and if the brothers' relationship can be helped. I also don't know if Rick has been authorized by his brothers to seek help. I run the risk of the two brothers casting me as Rick's man. Furthermore, Rick has asked me to advise him personally on a matter that could have grave consequences for the entire company.

Although I make no formal commitments, the engagement actually begins with my data collection during this first call. My first step is to get the names and birth dates of the brothers, any other siblings, and the parents. This information enables me to put each of them into the context of their respective stages of individual development.

Rick is the youngest. His father, the founder, was my client until his death seven years ago. Rick explains that the business problems began when one brother, Hal, went to Europe to start a plant to supply product to a European automotive manufacturer. Rick describes Hal as a spendthrift who is committing significant funds without informing his brothers or getting their authorization for the capital. I make note that there are issues here regarding financial controls. In addition, I wonder if the European project was well planned with budgetary projections and scheduled cash requirements; a responsible firm does not build a plant in Europe on a whim.

I ask Rick to describe his brother's professional skills. He reports, "Competent, but. . . ." I jot down "competent" and wonder what Hal is doing that has Rick so concerned.

Still not making any commitment to take the case, my next step is to review my consultative procedure with Rick. I explain that if hired, I will begin by individually interviewing all three brothers to gather information and perspectives about the family, the business, and the issues. Then I will conduct a family seminar that will include spouses, mother, a brother who left the business twelve years earlier, and all children age fourteen and older. (The inclusion of the entire family will help me enter the system as a neutral party and not as Rick's personal advocate.) At the start of the seminar I will explain how my involvement began, telling everyone about Rick's search, his call to me, and subsequent conversations with the two brothers who are owners. (Because I never know what kind of communications exist in a family, I always include everyone so that they all hear the same message, unfiltered through a family member.) This seminar will not focus on the issues of the family. My task for the day will be to present some useful information and to assess whether I can be of assistance to the brothers. The brothers' task will be to decide if I am the appropriate professional to assist them. The decision to engage me will have to be mutually agreeable to all the brothers and to me. During the course of the day there will be plenty of opportunity for everyone to ask questions, clarify points, and test perceptions.

A family business member is not likely to approach a professional advisor, no matter which discipline, for help with a broad family or business problem. It is more likely for one family business member to go to an advisor for help with a specific matter, such as a financial, legal, or tax question. Consider this same hypothetical case of the three brothers. Instead of calling a family business consultant, Rick goes to Charlie Baker, attorney and family systems–informed expert, for legal advice about exercising a put to sell his share of the family business to his brothers. Rick viewed and presented the problem in a narrow fashion: "Here is the situation, what should I do?" A client expects advisors to target their advice to the problem as the client perceives it.

But things are often not so simple. Although many clients' problems can be resolved by the practice of one's own discipline and professional area, a good number of the dilemmas brought to advisors are not so easily resolved. As the case illustrates, often the problem the client presents is not the real issue, runs deeper than the client thinks, or cannot be solved using only the skills of the expert's professional discipline. Even if Charlie chooses to address only the narrow issue that Rick presented, the odds are low, given the tension and anger simmering between the brothers, that they will be able to get past their emotional issues to negotiate the value of Rick's shares and the terms of his selling out.

The problem clients present is often only the tip of the iceberg. A specific issue concerning a family conflict, a succession dilemma, or a capitalization or legal need leads advisors into the tangled web of the family and the business.

The skills that we describe in this book will enable you to wrestle with the problems underneath the problem your clients present. As you will see, you often need to become more involved in the family and its affairs than you may expect. You will have to inquire into matters that you may consider personal. You may have to bring family members into discussions of difficult, emotional issues. The outcome will depend a great deal on the following rules, which should be established before assessing, let alone designing a solution to, the family business client's problems.

Entering the System as a Neutral Party

In order to help clients shift their perception of a problem from a narrow to a broader context, you need to help them view you somewhat differently than the expected norm. The steps that Charlie Baker must take to ensure his entry into the system as a neutral party contrast sharply with the way in which professionals usually work with a family and a family business client. They often do not know how to negotiate a neutral entry because they are already part of the system.

Charlie Baker had been involved with the family and with the business. He had been the personal lawyer and corporate counsel for the father when the boys were in their teens. He had drafted the father's will, handled important patent matters, and basically attended to all the father's personal and business legal matters. When the father died, Charlie Baker, along with Hal and the third brother, Ted, had administered the estate. The process went smoothly.

Over the years the brothers kept in intermittent contact with Charlie. Whenever differences between Hal, Ted, and Rick emerged, each privately sought out Charlie's advice. He always counseled patience and encouraged them to try to work things out. Until the call from Rick, Charlie had felt ineffective because the problems persisted. But this crisis represented a turning point. It inspired Charlie, who had been learning more about process consulting and family systems, to reenter the system as a neutral party. He accomplished this by redefining his role and being proactive in the manner described in the excerpt.

Redefining the Professional Role

Because of the multiple roles he had played over the years with this family business, Charlie Baker represented a valuable resource to the family. His years of association with the family and the firm added to his expert knowledge. He knew the company and the brothers well.

But to be effective in resolving this issue, Charlie had to redefine his role *for this intervention only*. His new role is one of facilitator or process consultant. He explained that he was there to bring about satisfactory resolution so the company could go forward in a strong, productive manner and not be torn by differences among the owners. He explained that he would not take a personal position on any of the issues that arose. If the brothers agreed to allow him to serve in this role, then Charlie would move forward for he would have negotiated a new contract within the system that allowed him to function as a knowledgeable third party and direct the brothers through a process that could lead to resolution of their issues.

Taking a Proactive Stance

Charlie had been aware of the growing animosity between the brothers as one by one each sought his advice. After the second brother came to him and certainly after Rick's call, Charlie knew he could have called a meeting of the brothers. Charlie did so now.

Being proactive and seeking out the brothers was a departure from Charlie's usual stance of responding to client-initiated requests. Professionals are often uncomfortable taking action in this way because it represents a redefinition of their role. They fear getting into conflict with the client or getting caught in the system.

At the outset of the meeting, Charlie set the stage and defined the task. He stated that through private conversations with each of the brothers he had become aware of some issues that had to be resolved.

Conducting Individual Interviews

Once Charlie obtained the brothers' consent to function in the role of process consultant, he needed to collect the facts. This can best be done on a one-on-one basis in private interviews.

Sorting Facts from Fiction and Perception. The data collection process is *not* like the fact finding a lawyer does in preparing for a courtroom case. Thus Charlie did not attempt to sketch a precise historical picture. His task was to determine what each brother believed were the facts. After all, most often it is not fact or reality that counts but rather what people *think* is fact or reality. People operate on their perceptions, not on the facts. Only through shared learning can perspectives change.

Charlie wrote all the perceived facts down on paper, without identifying who presented each one. It is important to label the list correctly: perceived facts. This process will highlight any conflicting perceptions.

Eliciting Best Outcomes. As part of each interview, Charlie asked each brother what, in his opinion, would be the best outcome from the problem-solving process. No matter how hard a brother sought Charlie's concurrence, Charlie was very careful not to give his opinion. It was even necessary for him to tell a brother that this was his stance in order not to be drawn toward one side or the other. Charlie's role was merely to orchestrate the process.

Charlie wrote each stated best outcome on a single piece of paper. In all likelihood, they all said something similar—to have the business run smoothly and maximize the return, perhaps. Having general agreement on the best outcome is very important because it is against these statements that all outcomes will be compared. Now Charlie was ready for the problem-solving session.

Holding the Initial Problem-Solving Session

The purpose of the initial session is to generate a shared sense of the issues. When this happens, problems are relatively easy to resolve.

Reviewing Best Outcomes. Charlie asked the brothers to look at the respective statements and determine if the statements, taken either individually or as a body, did represent the best outcomes for the company. Generally, even feuding family members can find common ground and agree on these points. Sometimes it is necessary to fine-tune the statement so that all can agree but because the best outcome is not likely to be the source of the problem this is usually a straightforward process.

This step sets the stage for a win-win outcome. Charlie locked the brothers into a best outcome that would serve as an objective criteria for measuring the efficacy of any proposed action.

Clarifying Perceived Facts.   At this point in the process, Charlie posted the perceived facts as he understood them. He invited the brothers to read the list and ask questions for clarification. There is a good chance that the perceived facts spark some fundamental mis- understandings. When these cropped up, Charlie asked, "Are there any points that need further clarification?" and then waited for the discussion to begin. As the moderator, Charlie carefully led the dis- cussion and kept the brothers focused on clarification.

This is often a good time to introduce some principles to help family members step back and reflect on how they do things. In this case, Charlie presented the four rules of Basque wisdom that are very applicable to this kind of family business discussion.

1. Show up. (If you don't show up, rules 2 through 4 don't apply!)
2. Pay attention to everything.
3. Tell the truth without blame or judgment.
4. Be open to outcomes rather than attached to one outcome.

Charlie could call on these principles if one brother began to blame or judge another or if one became locked into a single outcome.

Identifying Individual Perceptions.   After the process of clarifi- cation was complete, Charlie asked each of the brothers to write a brief statement describing the problem as he saw it. This process forced each one to crystallize his thinking and articulate it in such a way that it could be discussed by the group.

Group agreement on the definition of the problem is a prerequisite to all problem solving. When a group's members share an objective and agree about a presenting problem, they can almost always find a solution. So, after the brothers wrote their statements, Charlie asked them each to read them. Then there was a discussion. (We are all conditioned to take information through our eyes rather than through our ears. Simply writing a statement for all to read can lead to immediate clarification of misunderstandings.) Charlie looked for agreement on definition of the problem. If there is disagreement, there is need for more discussion or further refinement. Several problems may need to be addressed.

Predicting Outcomes from the Options. Businessmen and businesswomen predict the future daily based on some set of data. Stocks are bought and sold, new products are brought to market, personnel decisions are made. Through the process described, Charlie brought the brothers to a new definition of the problem. Then the task was to identify all the possible responses. To do this, Charlie created a grid with one column titled *Possible Response* and a second *Predicted Outcome*. Together with the brothers, Charlie listed all the possible responses, including doing nothing. Then he asked the brothers to predict the outcome based on each listed response. After this, he asked them to return to their stated best outcome and determine which, if any, of the predicted outcomes and possible responses most nearly fit. Exhibit 2.1 describes the process.

This process defused the issue, depersonalized the response to it, and put the brothers in the position of having to make a public decision based on what they had all agreed were the best outcomes. At no point did Charlie Baker offer his opinion on the matter; he was simply a facilitator and process consultant.

Charlie had one remaining task. He had to ask, "What has to be done to implement your decision?" When the brothers had

Exhibit 2.1. Mapping Problems, Outcomes, Responses.

The problem:

The brothers have different expectations about how to manage the capital investment program in the various divisions. Each brother feels proprietary and protective of his jurisdiction.

Stated best outcome:

Operate the business according to sound business practice, informing partners of major financial and management decisions in each division, setting a ceiling for each brother's financial expenditures, creating and abiding by budgetary projections.

Possible response:	Predicted outcome:
Do nothing.	Relationships will further deteriorate; Rick's anxiety will increase.
Establish tight budget.	Hal may comply with it or exceed it.
Increase information flow between brothers.	Rick's anxiety will be reduced *if* information shows all are within budget and if the information is accurate.
Send Rick to European division to work with Hal on budget process so he feels fully informed.	Rick's anxiety may diminish when he understands the start-up process *or* Hal may feel uncomfortable, threatened.
Let Rick leave.	Other brothers would lose the benefit of Rick's financial expertise, but they may feel a certain amount of relief from Rick's overbearing presence.

discussed their options and made their decision on implementation, he asked the brothers to comment on how they felt about the process, if it had helped them, and if they might find it useful once again in the future. (There is no substitute for positive reinforcement of a productive outcome—the opportunity should always be seized!)

Returning to the Original Role

When the meeting was over, Charlie stated that he was no longer in the process consulting role and was returning to his traditional function as corporate counsel. Charlie knew he had risked moving from the black-and-white arena of clear client definition into the gray. He hadn't given advice or gone to court, acted for suitor or defendants, or given an expert opinion. Instead, he had assumed the role of a proactive process consultant who guides the stakeholders to find their own solution.

Some professionals are trained to think and act on behalf of an individual client and they see a conflict if they take on more than one. But avoiding the interests of other stakeholders may lead to situations that force advisors to act in an adversarial way. As we mentioned in Chapter One, we believe it is wise to look for the common ground that allows stakeholders to achieve a win-win outcome. Of course, in some cases, advisors may encounter issues that pose a direct conflict between individual interests. If it is impossible to help the primary client work his or her way through that, it may ultimately be necessary for each party to have independent representation.

But suppose Charlie had not taken a proactive stance and not called that first meeting. Suppose the brothers had not reached agreement and Rick had exercised his put. Another scenario would have unfolded. Brother would have been pitted against brother. Thus we believe that the roles of professionals must ebb and flow with the circumstances and that the canons that govern the different professions must be flexible enough to support appropriate behavior.

Summary

In this chapter we presented some details about the different degrees of conflict a family may present and the different styles of advising that a professional can employ. As the conflict level in a system rises, expert skills are harder to use unless they are informed by a broader awareness.

We talked about the process of defining, redefining, and renegotiating one's role as one begins any phase of work with a family business. When professionals change their role or begin to do different things with a family, they need to be clear and explicit about what is happening.

Process consulting skills are a useful addition to any professional's repertoire in a family business situation or in any situation where the interests of different parties are at odds. These skills enable advisors to move out of their expert role, conduct an inquiry into the nature of a difficulty, and convene the family for exploration of an issue.

Chapter Three

Navigating the Dynamics
of the Family in Business

The family business begins as a family, with its own unique set of
rules, values, and methods of communication, all of which affect
the business, either positively or negatively. In addition, the individual members of the family have unique personalities and each
progresses through fairly predictable stages that also affect how they
work together in the business. Advisors must understand the complex nature of the systems of business and family in order to provide
assistance to the business. Indeed, many of the difficulties of the
business stem from issues in the family. The advisor who tries only
to deal with the business dimension of a dilemma may find that
things just don't get resolved.

    This chapter presents what we call the *family systems perspec-
tive*, a model to help advisors understand and work within the
dynamic structures of the family and the business and the some-
times-baffling gray areas in which they intersect. The model applies
the core principles of process consulting that we outlined in Chapter One:

- Define the family business system as the client.
- Work with whole family and business systems.
- Balance the needs of all stakeholders.
- Open up communication.
- Create clear structures and boundaries.
- Help the family business and the people within it to grow and
  change.

In order to apply these core principles, you will need some background information. We present conceptual tools to help you assess several important factors, including each family member's stage in life, the family communication patterns, and the family's placement on a scale that rates qualities of successful business families.

Conceptual Tool One:
Getting Comfortable in the Gray Zones

We do not advocate that professionals who work with family businesses become psychologists. However, we do recommend that they become grounded in relevant models from individual psychology and family systems theory so they can identify and anticipate sensitive areas as they work with family business clients.

A system is an interconnected set of parts that act as if they were a single whole. These parts may be printed circuits, clouds and the atmospheric conditions that produce our weather, or a group of people such as a family. Systems theory teaches that all aspects (or subsystems) of a system are interdependent. In other words, what affects one part affects the others. Further, when a problem cannot be resolved at one level of the system it must be addressed at another. The problems of the family business cannot be addressed by looking at the business or its finances alone; an intervention must also include the family.

The family and the business, while containing many of the same people, are vastly different worlds. Each has its own priorities, goals, and expectations. One world involves emotional acceptance; the other demands rationality and results. The challenge for a family business is learning how to shift the relationship as family members move between the two systems. Rules, expectations, and behaviors must all shift.

The two systems are pictured as overlapping circles in Figure 3.1. We have found this illustration useful in our work with families in business to help them visualize the dynamics of their situation. It often helps them understand the conflicts they are experiencing.

Figure 3.1. Intersecting Family Business Systems.

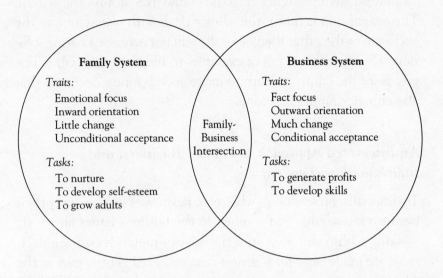

Family System

Traits:
    Emotional focus
    Inward orientation
    Little change
    Unconditional acceptance

Tasks:
    To nurture
    To develop self-esteem
    To grow adults

Family-
Business
Intersection

Business System

Traits:
    Fact focus
    Outward orientation
    Much change
    Conditional acceptance

Tasks:
    To generate profits
    To develop skills

The two circles represent the interlocking systems that together form a third system, the family business. The family system has particular needs and energies that are sometimes at odds with the business system. The family system seeks to preserve harmony and minimize change; in contrast, the business system sometimes requires conflict and change. The tasks of the two systems are very different, too. The family exists to develop, nurture, and care for its members; the business seeks to generate profits and act effectively in a competitive environment. In fact, many of the dilemmas of the family business come when family needs or priorities overwhelm the business's needs. Problems inevitably erupt when a family member expects people in the business realm to operate by the rules used in the family realm or vice versa.

The intersection of the circles in the figure represents the areas involving decisions and problems that have ramifications for both the family and the business. The goal for a family business advisor is to help the family develop the skills to work in that area where family and business intersect, to set up, clarify, or develop relationships in that area. In effect, the advisor must develop a process awareness, paying attention to the boundaries around the system. The assumption is that if the advisor deals with one system to the exclusion of the other then he or she will not achieve a lasting solution. The literature is full of examples to illustrate this point. The goal is for the family to learn to make good business decisions that also enhance family harmony.

An Integrated Approach to Family, Business, and Individual Development

Traditionally, professionals who serve businesses seek to apply their business knowledge and acumen to the business issues alone. By working within this area only, the advisor pretends business decisions are made only for business reasons. That is only part of the story. Business patterns and practices are deeply influenced by the reality of the family system.

Advisors must focus not only on the elements in the business area but also on the dynamics that underpin all three circles shown in Figure 3.2: family stages, individual stages, and business stages of development. The art of family business consulting comes from learning how all three interacting circles become a "window on a family" through which advisors can gain a more comprehensive understanding of unresolved business problems.

The three subsystems—the family, the business, and the individuals—all have their own needs, goals, and stages of development. When all three systems are in harmony, conflict is at a minimum. But it is rare that these systems are in harmony. One of the most frequent sources of conflict is a collision between individuals at different stages of development, each with different goals, needs, and tolerance for risk. In the following sections, we will briefly describe the developmental stages of each system and suggest references should you wish to learn more about their development.

Figure 3.2. The Integrated View of Family,
Individual, and Business Stages of Development.

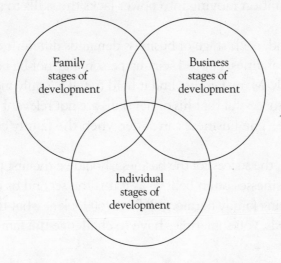

Business Stages of Development

Businesses grow, develop, thrive, and decline just as people and families do. However, their timetables are not biological even though some theorists have tried to define clear, limited stages of business development.

Most models of business development look like an S curve. First there is the start-up phase when the business is born in the mind of the entrepreneur. Then there is the stage when the business becomes successful and grows quickly; this stage can last for several years. Finally, the growth levels off and can even suddenly decline if the business fails to renew itself with a new product, idea, or plan; this is when many businesses fail or are acquired. Many need new capitalization or management.

Several aspects of these stages of development can affect family business advisors. First, the stages a business progresses through are not necessarily in sync with the family's or an individual's stages of development. That is, a business may need renewal or revitalization just when its founder wants to harvest the fruits of his years of work. Or a business may need renewal and change but the new generation moving into power lacks the skills to accomplish this.

Second, each stage of business demands different managerial skills and abilities. A good start-up person may not be best to manage growth. Many families find it hard to tell a family member who has been successful that his or her skills are not relevant to the new challenge. The business can suffer when the family cannot face reality.

Third, the success of the business should be the first priority. Yet family businesses often behave as if it is the second or third priority, following family harmony. When you look at what the business really needs, you sometimes have to challenge the family's way of working.

For a thorough discussion of the stages of business development, see *Smart Growth: Critical Choices for Business Growth and Prosperity* (Poza, 1989).

Family Stages of Development

There are several major challenging phases in a family's development: the couple, the family with small children, the family with teenage children, the empty nest, the retirees, the widow or widower.

Every family goes through the phases in a different rhythm. Today, families may go through them in a somewhat different order or more than once, resulting in additional complex layers of the family business system. Each phase of family development has its own unique joys and challenges. For the new couple, establishing a rhythm together is a great challenge. Developing trust and understanding, working through differences in lifestyles and habits, and merging the cultures they bring from their families of origin are important tasks. The person entering a business family may find, for example, that he or she is marrying a business and taking on a new set of responsibilities.

The family with young children faces the challenge of growing into the role of parenting, learning how to juggle caring for baby with being a couple and running a business. Sleep deprivation is a side effect at this stage!

Parenting a teenager rivals being a teenager as the most difficult stage of life. Learning how to balance letting go and setting boundaries, seeking togetherness and leaving space, allowing rebellion and allowing independence are all challenges for both generations. The way that teenagers learn about the business sets the stage for later dramas and challenges and affects personal development. (We will see more about this in Chapter Nine.)

When the family is in the empty nest stage, there may be a tremendous sense of loss, sense of relief, or both. The focus of the couple may revert to themselves after having been on the children. This can be a period of satisfying intimacy or a time to face its absence. (In fact, this stage is one of the most frequent periods of divorce.) Significant role adjustments occur at this time.

The couple makes its next major adjustment as one or both face retirement and perhaps even more time together. At this time or thereafter, most couples face their own mortality or widowhood.

It is important for advisors to keep the life phases in mind, particularly when they look at the interface of the needs of the family and the needs of the business; we will discuss this in more detail in the following section. (For an in-depth look at work with families at each stage, see *Reweaving the Family Tapestry* [Brown, 1991].) The family and business members' priorities often shift from one family stage to the next. For example, sometimes empty nesters feel a surge of freedom and want to spend some time traveling. If the business can accommodate the individual's absence, these family needs may be met.

At some point after the children have grown something happens to cause a family to review the dynamics of their collective and individual relationships. They may find themselves in a crisis or simply try to make an improvement for an unrelated reason. Many times the need for planning for business succession forces them to consider how well the business is doing. Many families realize that things are not as they had hoped yet know neither what caused the difficulties nor how to commence the improvement effort. Understanding the dynamics of family development is a first step.

Most families follow a fairly typical pattern during the early child-rearing years. Both parents and children experience a number of psychological bumps and bruises. As children enter adolescence their striving for independence begins a process of individuation that proceeds in definable stages. This process is critical to family members' ability to work effectively within a family business.

A family member who has not completed the process of healthy individuation is much more difficult to work with. Healthy individuation means that the individual has a clear sense of identity that is independent of the people surrounding him or her. Such people have well-defined personal values that allow them to react to many situations with integrity. If they are challenged, they are confident and react assertively (rather than passively giving up their perspective or aggressively insisting that everyone else adopt it). They have healthy interpersonal boundaries. In other words, their boundaries are "permeable." They allow input into their thinking but are not consumed or excessively influenced by others. They are caring and concerned about others but not obsessed with addressing others' needs to the extent that their own needs are overwhelmed.

When people are not well individuated, they tend to overreact to what relatives say. They are often excessively defensive or hypersensitive to feedback or criticism and take things too personally. This is the cause of much of the interpersonal conflict that occurs in family businesses.

The first phase in the individuation process is characterized by "breaking away." Many children become rebellious and do things that jeopardize their relationships with their parents. In late adolescence, children tend to grow apart psychologically and emotionally as they leave home to pursue their own individual quests. Most families come back together—physically at least—as the children enter their mid-twenties. However, since these families have grown apart, they have difficulty reconnecting as adults. This is especially true if the parents have divorced and remarried in the interim. Although some families stay positively connected through the adolescent years, most do not. Thus they need to reconnect, to reestablish some elements of the close emotional relationships that existed earlier but were damaged by time and events. Parents and children have to determine how to relate as adults rather than as parent and child.

For some individuals, earlier relationships may have been neither positive nor healthy; they may even have been dysfunctional. A child's relationship with a parent may have been dominated by a dependency that was outgrown and left behind at some point. Parents may have unknowingly expected their children to achieve their own unfulfilled desires. The father who pushes his son to accomplish more as an athlete than he did is an example. In such cases, the previous relationship needs to be replaced with a better, healthier relationship.

Reconnecting is not easy. Most families have great difficulty doing it and often need outside help. Unless the family reconnects, individuals lose a tremendous opportunity for satisfying and meaningful adult relationships. More to the point in this discussion, a family in business that has not reconnected is an accident waiting to happen.

Individual Stages of Development

We alluded to some of the challenges of individual development during our discussion of adolescent development. Social scientists and psychologists have only begun to study adult development in recent years (see *Seasons of a Man's Life* [Levinson, 1978]). But we have found that some of the dilemmas faced in family business consulting are caused by the stage of development of one or more family members connected with the business. Each stage has its own challenges and tasks. Table 3.1 adapts Levinson's model to present the life challenge that each age and stage needs to address.

Again, it is important to note that the stages of family life, individual development, and business growth are rarely synchronized. The challenges family business advisors face may stem from conflicts in development between the subsystems and between individuals.

When family members work together they tend blithely to assume that the others are operating at their own individual stages of development. Obviously, this is not the case. Two people are rarely in the same stage of growth, and certainly not when they are members of different generations.

Table 3.1. Challenges of Individual Stages of Adult Development.

Age	Stage	Challenge
17–22	Transition to early adult	Form a dream, have mentor relationships and occupations.
22–28	Entry into adult world	Explore the possibilities of the world.
28–33	Age 30 transition	Form love relationships.
33–40	Settling-down phase	Become one's own person; become successful.
40–45	Midlife transition	Come to terms with one's limitations.
45–50	Beginning of midadulthood	Commit to new or reaffirm old choices
50–55	Age 50 transition	Create the legacy.
55–60	Ending of midadulthood	Sustain youth while facing bodily decline.
60–65	Late adult transition	Pass on authority.
60–80+	Late adulthood	Find integrity in one's life.

One of the principal tasks of one's twenties is to explore career options and to settle on one. Between the ages of twenty-two and thirty, the typical American can expect to explore between three and seven distinct careers. This may take the form of a smooth progression through a single discipline characterized by increasing levels of responsibility and a tighter focus on one aspect of a career. Or the pattern may be characterized by false starts and half starts as the individual tries first one field and then another until a focus comes into view. Neither pattern is superior; it is reaching a single career focus that is important. However, one way or the other the individual must develop the fire in the belly for the work he or she does and focus on achieving success in that arena. This is why it is valuable for a family to encourage extensive job experience outside of the family enterprise before allowing members to be employed within it. Some families inadvertently place a great value on cohesion even though letting go for the sake of outside exploration might bring new and exciting ideas and more expertise into the family business at a later date.

Interconnection of the Developmental Phases

Some years ago one family business consultant interviewed a fifty-seven-year-old man who was in charge of the finances of his family's chain of a dozen funeral homes. In the course of the interview the man burst into tears, stating, "I never wanted to come into this business in the first place. My family insisted on it." Forces in the family had prevented him from completing the developmental stage of exploring career options. At fifty-seven he had to admit that he had not chosen the career he might have wished.

Sometimes developmental stages in all circles are in harmony with one another, at other times they are in conflict. When children reach their early twenties, their parents, often in their forties, are willing to serve as mentors. As both generations move up a decade, they may drift apart; this is a normal phenomenon in the mentor-mentee relationship. By one's early to mid-thirties, most adults often think they have learned enough from their parent-mentors and are ready and eager to be in charge of some part of their work lives. They no longer need their parent-mentors who, by now in their mid-fifties, are themselves likely to want firm control of their careers and business lives. Thus they are both on track developmentally but there is a good chance that control will be an issue between them. Solutions must address both their needs; perhaps parts of the business can be spun off or a new division acquired or launched so that all can all flex their muscles.

Let's look at an example. Soon after the Smiths were married, Mr. Smith started his own plumbing supply business. Mrs. Smith helped by doing the books and answering the telephone. When their first son was born, Mrs. Smith stopped working to stay home with him. Mr. Smith replaced her by hiring an office manager. In the next five years, Mr. Smith added a plumbing supply division and the couple had another child. As both the business and the children grew, Mrs. Smith occasionally pinch-hit in the office or assisted with inventory. By the time the children were seven or eight, they regularly came to the store to help out. When they grew older, during summer vacations the son worked with the plumbers and the daughter filled orders at the supply counter.

After graduating high school, the son wanted to follow in his father's footsteps and joined his father in the business. The daughter had little interest in it and went on to college, only helping out at the business to make extra money. When the children left home, Mrs. Smith, now forty-four, wanted to become more involved with the business. She had reached both the midlife transition stage (her individual life stage) and the empty nest stage (her family stage). It should be noted that we don't refer to the former as a midlife crisis because a "crisis" can be avoided if, when people pass through this predictable phase, they have the skills to readjust the dream about life and career they had in their twenties to the realities of their life experiences. In Mrs. Smith's case, having completed her full-time job as mother and feeling a void, she looked to the business to fill the void although there was no clear role for her at that time.

How about the others? The son, now twenty-three, wanted to do things his own way and establish himself as an independent adult. He was at the "entering adult world" stage of his life. He sought Dad's acceptance and more power running the business but was not completely competent to do so. Dad, at forty-eight, was in the "entering middle adulthood" stage: he didn't yet fully trust his son's judgment and was afraid to leave his baby (the business) in his son's hands. Like many entrepreneurs, Mr. Smith had a tremendous need to control the business and found it difficult to trust others with it.

And the business? The business was moving through its own developmental stage, toward more delegation after an era of central control. The business had grown too big to be controlled solely at the top; the founder needed to delegate more responsibility. Controls had to be established to enable managers to handle delegated tasks responsibly while also allowing for the comfort of the control-minded founder. The skills needed to be an entrepreneur (controlling all aspects of the business) are antithetical to those needed to create a professionally managed business. Many entrepreneurs have great difficulty navigating through these business stages.

Thus, at this stage in their development there were several points of conflict between the individual, family, and business stages that created the conflicts experienced in the business and especially by Mr. Smith.

- The business needed systems and controls at its stage of development and none of the family (or employees) appeared able to establish them.
- The son was frustrated that his father was holding him back by retaining control and interpreted that as a vote of no confidence. Father and son bickered frequently; the father felt his son was disrespectful and unappreciative.

- Mother's development and the business's development were not in sync either. The business didn't need another clerical person. Furthermore, Mr. Smith had his wife on the payroll even though he knew it didn't make business sense. This created some morale problems for the nonfamily employees.

The Smiths' example helps us to understand how families in business together must keep their personal, family, and business agendas clear and separated. When family business owners feel that the business must address all the family needs and the family must address all the business needs, neither system is successful.

It is important to realize that developmental stages do not unfold according to chronological age. They flow sequentially as long as individuals are given the space and the tools to move from one stage to the next. As already mentioned, unresolved issues or traumas can impede development along the continuum. Unfinished business in one stage remains unfinished. Someday the task will have to be completed. In the case of the Smiths, if the father did not come to understand and accept his son's need for control over some aspect of the business, the son's development might slow and their relationship deteriorate. The constraints the father placed on the son would force the driving forces in the son's development to be expressed in ways that might be less than constructive. It might even cause the son to leave the business altogether, undermining one of the father's lifelong goals for business continuity.

It is often assumed that family members have common points of view simply because they are a family. In fact, this is frequently not the case.

Let us consider the case of three individuals: a man aged seventy-six, his son aged fifty-one, and his grandson aged twenty-seven. The man tells his son, "You are going to have to buy this business from me just as I bought it from my father's estate!" The son, who has worked diligently in the business for thirty years, feels that his father has suddenly undermined his previous work, is in the process of undermining his future establishment in the business, and, probably, has undermined the emotional bond that he thought existed between them. Meanwhile, the grandson also feels threatened, thinking, "If my father is treated this way, then is this the right place for me?" Each of these men brings a different viewpoint to the issue that was formed by the particular relationship involved and his own stage of life. Each has a reason for his particular thinking and course of action and the three may not necessarily agree on personal agendas. The three will look at any issue from the perspective of their own stage in life and of their own dynamics within the family system.

Identifying Strengths and Weaknesses in the Family System

When a family finds itself in trouble, its members rarely look to themselves to find the remedy. The family either blames one individual who exhibits behavior that goes against the family's rules—which may or may not conform to society's rules—or they blame an outside agency, the tax system or their advisor, for example. Although this may keep the family members from seeing their own roles in the problem, it is not an effective remedy for family problems.

A good starting point is to outline the characteristics of the family system. The following steps outline a good starting point for preventative work that anticipates problem areas:

1.   Clearly define the system's members. Who's in and who's out?

2.   Identify the system's prescribed set of rules or procedures for how members of the system function and interact with each other. What is the hierarchy? What are its unwritten and often unspoken roles and tasks? To what extent does the system resist change and efforts to change it?

3.   Identify where and how the family pattern of functioning supports and where and how it impedes sound business practices. What are the information collection and dissemination mechanisms

in the family? These family patterns will be transferred to the business. What are the decision-making procedures in the family and the business?

4.   Scout out successful methods of action and productive behaviors that members may have developed in environments outside the family system. Advisors may be able to use these successful methods of interaction as models for improved interactions within the family system. It's important to recognize, however, the vulnerability of all family members to be drawn back into the prevailing family style and not use the new behaviors. This type of regression occurs most frequently when an individual, several individuals, or system are under stress.

5.   Explore times in the past when the family worked together smoothly. What was done differently then, before stress, pressure, or conflict led the members to revert to original patterns? Help members learn how to circumvent the tendency to revert to less successful patterns.

One family's original pattern had been to delegate all decisions upward to the patriarch. However, family members learned that in effectively managed companies, decisions are delegated downward in the organizational structure and decided to operate their business in this manner. The business operated smoothly under ordinary conditions but as soon as pressures hit, all members reverted to the original pattern, severely handicapping effective decision making. A bottleneck developed in the decision-making process and morale declined as employees felt disempowered. As decisions failed to be made in a timely fashion, opportunities were lost and the business suffered.

Developing a Family Genogram

Gathering data is not always easy but there are techniques and tools that can help a consultant gain access to a family's patterns. One tool is the family genogram, sometimes called the family tree. It is used frequently in family assessment and has been codified by two generations of family therapists.

To make a genogram, begin with the business owner and spouse and then add all of the children, their spouses, and their grandchildren. Determine the date of birth for each person. With this complete, push the chart back one or two generations and try to fill in ancestors on both sides of the family. Figure 3.3 provides instructions for preparing a family genogram.

We recommend that advisors learn the process by drawing a genogram of their own family. This process not only gives practice but also provides insight into one's own family system and dynamics. This is helpful in minimizing the chances of projecting one's own family issues onto the client (a process that is called *countertransference*). Without self-understanding, advisors will be handicapped in their ability to understand the families they serve.

After completing the client's family genogram, fill in the following chart (Exhibit 3.1) by addressing each question.

The answers to the questions in the exhibit are certain to give further insight into the ways in which the family functions. It is quite likely that some patterns will emerge, such as the following:

- There are transfers of ownership from father to eldest son.
- There is emphasis on the work ethic.
- There is emphasis on education and competence.
- There is avoidance of conflict.
- There is late retirement with reluctance to release control.
- One gender (usually male) is given preferential treatment over the other.
- The eldest children are expected to be responsible for other children.
- Financial matters are never discussed openly so successors are ill informed.
- Parents fear that gifts of money have a deleterious impact on

Figure 3.3. Harwood Family Genogram.

Instructions:

1. Use squares for men ☐ and circles for women ◯ . Add ages.

2. Place the husband on the left and draw a solid line to the wife on the right.

3. Indicate marriage by the symbol m. and give the date.

    m. 1950

4. Indicate birth order of children from left to right. Include, if known, the following information:
    a. Full names and nicknames.
    b. Birth and death dates and locations.
    c. Dates of marriages and locations.

5. To indicate a person is deceased, put a cross through the symbol.

6. To indicate a divorce, use the symbol ⟨ d. through the marriage line. Show the date and the parent with custody of the children.

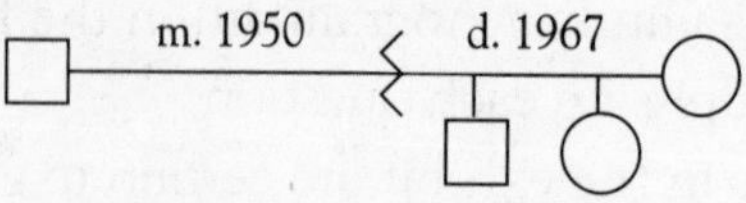

    m. 1950   ⟨ d. 1967

7. To indicate a second marriage or subsequent marriages, put the number of the marriage with the date.

    m. 1967   ⟨ d. 1969   m   2m. 1972

8. Indicate the number of years between siblings.

    Example:

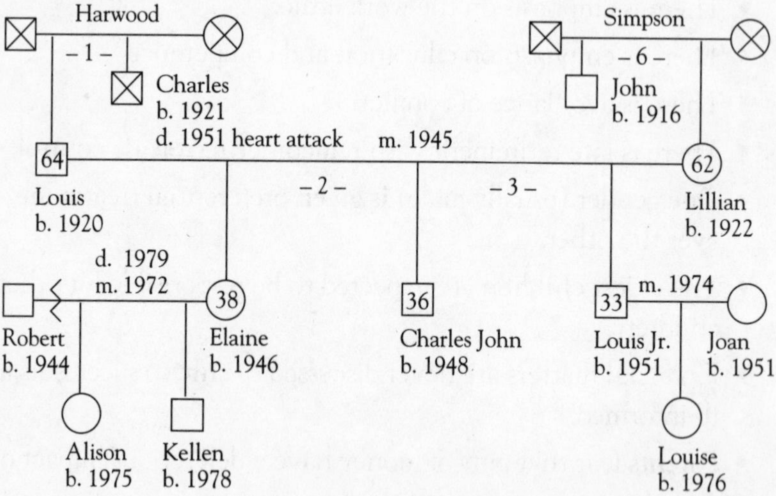

Exhibit 3.1. Implications of Family Behavior.

Question	Family Behavior	Implications: Potential Business Conflicts
How are decisions made?		
What activities are important to the family?		
Who takes after whom, who looks like whom?		
Are differences of opinion welcomed?		
How are differences resolved?		
How is money managed?		
Are finances openly discussed?		
How healthy are family members?		
What was the cause of death of ancestors and when did the death occur?		
Were there substantial assets in previous generations?		
How did previous generations handle their estates? Who were the recipients of any assets?		
Were there any secrets that were later disclosed? Who revealed them?		
How did/does this family react when a family member makes a mistake?		
Are there patterns of substance use or abuse or other compulsive disorders?		
Is greater value placed on children of one sex than the other? How is this made evident?		
How do individuals handle retirement? At what age did they retire? What do/did they do in retirement?		
What role does competition or competitive sports play in family interaction?		

the children so trust instruments control transferred assets well beyond the appropriate point.

- There are extreme expectations for high-level performance or following in parents' footsteps in school.
- There are high levels of competition among siblings or between parents and children.

The emergence of such patterns provides insight into the family messages, helps advisors understand the dynamics that may be governing the way the family and the business are functioning, and lends clues as to how best to proceed in the clients' interests.

It is often helpful to look into the generational sequence of the family. You may be surprised to learn that things that occurred several generations earlier are still having an influence. Family patterns often repeat themselves. For example, the eldest child may have dropped out of college at the same age in three successive generations or young children may have taken care of a parent in different generations. Furthermore, today you may very well be working with a "blended" family that brings its own set of dynamics and issues. Biological children against stepchildren, biological parents against stepparents: these are common sources of conflict. In addition, unresolved issues often exist between the biological parent and biological children after a divorce.

Another set of factors explain a family's interacting and functioning. These points include the following: How open and candid are discussions? Does a high level of trust exist? To what degree are there secrets? Who is told what? Do there seem to be cliques of individuals? How open is communication? What is the information flow? How connected or detached does the family seem to be as a group? How often do they get together as a family? Are these happy times, sad times, conflicting times? Who seems to be the informal leader? Are there any "black sheep" and why? Did any energy-consuming negative incidents occur in the past?

The answers to these questions will help advisors assess their clients as a family and their ability to work together as a team. To paraphrase the Bible, "The sins of the fathers and mothers are visited unto the sons and daughters for seven generations." The matter of patterns has been with us a very long time. When you find them, you are on the verge of important insights. When this occurs you can "wonder" with the clients about the significance of the pattern and explore their feelings about the patterns. Do they wish to continue the pattern or do they want it to stop? That question will often open up a discussion that leads to new clarity about the tasks that your client has asked you to perform.

Conceptual Tool Two: Identifying Communication Impediments

Communication is the currency of human systems. We can't operate within a system or move between systems without currency. Thus understanding family communication patterns is critical to working with a family business.

Overcoming "Undiscussables"

Twenty years of family history may have produced certain topics that are difficult to discuss. Examples are money, ownership, certain individuals, certain events, the rationale for decision making, and perceived injustices and shameful events. Such subjects represent enormous emotional and communicative black holes. Every family has "undiscussables" that are barriers to family members developing good relationships with one another. Curiously, when something is not discussed it takes on additional energy and gains in importance for the family.

Families vary tremendously in their ability to maintain open, direct, and positive lines of communication. Some do pretty well and only have trouble with a few topics. Others do reasonably well, solving mutual problems and making decisions. Yet others have difficulty talking about topics any more sensitive than the weather.

In many families an almost tangible feeling of "surfaceness" characterizes most interactions.

Avoiding touchy issues may superficially and tenuously maintain harmony and stability, but it has long-term costs, including disconnection and future misunderstandings. Families can learn to develop a forum with set ground rules to explore difficult topics. Ordinary family gatherings, however, are usually too informal and too unstructured for this to occur.

The advisor's job is to recognize any black holes that are blocking sound business practices and create a forum in which they can be worked through constructively. These are not easy tasks. Spotting something—actually, recognizing its absence—requires a certain degree of intuition and an ability to connect disparate signals and cues. Responding effectively can be even trickier. By definition, no one is comfortable addressing undiscussables. The risk of hurting sensitive feelings is high and people may not be able to overcome overriding fears. Earlier discussions on the subject may have had negative consequences. Few people are willing to risk repeating an unpleasant experience.

However, there are many approaches advisors can choose from. They can create a family forum that meets regularly (see Chapter Seven for more on this). They can recommend that the family hire a process specialist—such as a communications consultant, a psychologist, family therapist, or organization development consultant—to come in and facilitate a half-day session on improved communications. Accomplishing such a session requires special skill and experience that can't be learned simply by reading a book or experimenting on a family.

Avoiding Communication Triangles

Additional impediments to healthy communication are lack of direct communication and formation of triangles. Put simply, triangles occur when two people have tension in their relationship and have trouble communicating directly and seduce another person to accomplish the communication between them (see Figure 3.4). Most frequently, this go-between is enlisted as an aid to one or the other individual and the anger that that individual feels is transmitted to the go-between, who then tries to get the other party to change.

In a triangle, communication between the initial two people rarely improves. In fact, triangles tend to perpetuate a lack of direct communication. Furthermore, individuals who act as go-between often end up misunderstanding someone and exacerbating the situation. They may also alienate themselves from both parties.

If you spot a triangle in the family you are working with, it indicates an area where direct communication has been problematical and is worth exploring. (See Chapter Six for more suggestions.) We encourage advisors to stay out of triangles. To do so, we offer the following suggestions:

Figure 3.4. A Family Triangle.

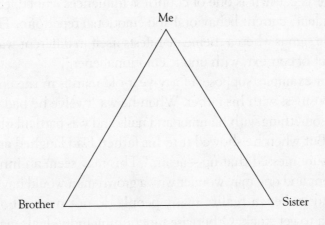

- Listen with empathy when someone vents a problem about a third party but don't jump in the middle.

- Be a coach: help the person who is coming to you to give constructive feedback to the third party.

- Remember that the person in the middle often "gets shot" by both sides and just perpetuates a dysfunctional relationship.

- Don't become a go-between carrying family messages from one person to another under any circumstances.

Thawing Frozen Emotional Issues

Families often have difficulty if an emotional issue has been frozen in the past and not allowed to come forward and run its course. This can be particularly true when the issue involves a death. Often surviving family members have not worked through their grief or the unresolved issues they had with the deceased person. Although the issue is "history" the individual continues to be affected by it in the present.

What can be done in the present to make amends for something that happened in the past is not usually clear. The situation is like an itch that cannot be scratched. This type of issue is hard to spot because it is one of countless influences embedded in the individual's current behavioral and emotional repertoire. The most telltale sign is when a theme manifests itself in different ways, usually out of context, with undue emotional energy.

For example, suppose a forty-year-old man is in the construction business with his father. When he was twelve he had tried to build something with hammer and nails and was particularly proud of it. But when he showed it to his father, Dad laughed and said, "You sure messed that up—again." This may seem an innocuous incident and one may wonder why a grown man would have to get beyond it. Yet in reality many people do not need a bona fide trauma to get stuck. Otherwise functioning individuals may enter adulthood burdened by childhood insecurities, resentments, and sibling rivalries that may at times turn them into children.

It is important to understand that an individual may not be aware of a frozen emotional issue. When a child has a frozen emotional problem with a parent who has passed away, the possibility for successful resolution is greatly diminished because that person is not available to work it out with. This is the time for the individual to work with a trained clinical professional.

The first step toward resolution is to initiate a discussion focused on the point in time that the incident occurred. The forty-year-old construction worker may not realize he is "stuck" at age twelve as far as this particular event is concerned. The advisor must be aware that the resentment of the twelve-year-old could be transferred to the advisor, who may be seen as an authority figure. As a result, the advisor must exercise caution in the process of helping the forty-year-old get "unstuck." An effective approach would be to point out patterns spotted and suggest that the family may be stuck with an old issue that is being replayed in the present. Giving examples of what was seen may be the piece of the puzzle such an individual needs to address the problem himself or to become motivated to seek further help.

More problems develop when an unresolved issue is transferred from a family to the business. For example, one family extended the pattern of taking care of their younger brother, the baby in the family, when he entered the business. His older brothers looked out for him by not giving him real responsibilities and not expecting much from him. He continued his part of the pattern by being an irresponsible clown and acting like a child. The family pattern had damaging effects on the business. The family pattern also impeded this individual's movement. An advisor might have given the man specific jobs and held him accountable. If that can't happen in a family business then such an individual shouldn't be part of it.

An effective way to have broached this subject would have been to indicate that in most situations the man demonstrated sound business judgment but in several areas he seemed conflicted and reacted impulsively or emotionally. The advisor could then have given an example of this kind of behavior.

Balancing Confrontation and Fairness

Families often have difficulty resolving issues because individuals are not very skilled at productive confrontation and conflict resolution. They draw on models they developed in childhood that have taught them either to "gunnysack" a concern or to explode. It is difficult to begin to clarify conflicts and rebuild relationships when family members can't constructively confront sensitive issues.

Many disagreements between family members revolve around the issue of fairness. Children grow up expecting to be treated fairly within the family but develop unrealistic expectations about what that means that continue into adulthood.

Even though these rules about fairness and expected treatment are unspoken, they become norms within the family. Each child learns to apply them astutely in any given situation. Each of us probably grew up with unrealistic expectations of what our parents should give us. These expectations become magnified in a family business where money and other assets are to be distributed equitably—though not necessarily equally—at some point. An advisor can be of tremendous service by pointing out that fair does not necessarily mean equal when it comes to job performance, responsibility, and compensation.

Conceptual Tool Three: Rating a Client on a Scale of Successful Family Businesses

In every occupation or profession there are a set of qualities and behaviors that characterize a successful person. The same is true of families. Based on our experiences we have established a set of qualities and behaviors that characterize the family that remains both positively connected and successfully in business. The profile contrasts markedly with that of enmeshed families (which allow no emotional boundaries between members) and dysfunctional families (which intentionally or inadvertently have a negative impact on individual members and the family unit as a whole). To be successful, a family must have all of the qualities to some degree. The greater the degree the better. The qualities are described in the following paragraphs.

Shared Values

If there is basic agreement about underlying values then it is possible for a family to create a shared vision of itself and of business's future that all family members can pursue harmoniously.

With this in mind, the advisor should address the following questions: To what extent does the family share core values, especially about people, work, and money? What are the main sources of conflict? Who did or did not do what, spend how much, get paid more, work as hard or at least do his share, hire or fire so and so?

Shared Power

Thomas Jefferson notwithstanding, all men and women are not created equally. We all have different strengths, talents, and abilities. But sharing does not require strict equality. To what extent do family members share power across generations, between spouses, among siblings?

Families that learn to respect one another's competencies and expertise defer to the family member that has the expertise in a given area. A family that attempts to do everything equally for each child is most likely to develop problems of power. It is important that individuals recognize that it is okay to have an opinion on everything but not okay to expect it to prevail at all times.

At the dinner table, parents make sure that Johnny, Billy, Mary, and Beth all are given equal time. Each child is encouraged to have opinions, a process that goes a long way toward building self-esteem. But an expectation of complete equality on all matters can be disastrous when carried into the business by adults working together.

Shared Traditions

What makes the family special and sets it apart from all other families? Some families play, practice religious ceremonies, travel together, or always eat cranberry sauce on their pumpkin pie. Others always spend their Christmas holiday at Aspen.

Whatever the tradition, it has the effect of bonding the family members into a unit that makes them unique. Ongoing traditions maintain and strengthen the bonds.

Willingness to Learn and Grow

Is the family open to new ideas and new approaches? Those who are can solve virtually any problem.

Considering another point of view and a different orientation allows for identification of the crevice in any problem, making it possible to crack it open and find a solution. The family that is open to new ideas sees positive possibilities in the most negative situations; this is a fundamental requirement for effective problem solving.

Group Activities

To what extent do family members maintain their sense of humor and demonstrate the ability to have fun, be playful with each other, and play together? When families put this kind of "relationship currency" into the family bank they build a reserve to draw upon during times of disagreement.

The family whose business is its only form of interaction is a family waiting to polarize around some business issue.

Expressions of Genuine Caring

How openly do family members express feelings of concern for one another? How do members know if others really care about them? One indication of genuine caring is the degree to which they give others their undivided attention.

Genuine caring may be expressed by making a phone call simply "to visit," stopping for a cup of coffee, sending a post card, offering an invitation to a movie, or taking a relative's children for a weekend so the parents have some time off. All are examples of expressions of caring.

Mutual Respect and Trust

Trust is built on a history of keeping one's word, doing what one says one will do. Of course trust is at the foundation of any healthy long-term relationship, not just those in family businesses. Where can you identify trust and respect among family members?

Trust that is built over years between and among family members in business is a glue that binds. Some might even call it love.

Assistance and Support for One Another

Are family members "there" for one another, especially at times of grief, loss, pain, and shame? No one can go through life without experiencing these emotions. How the extended family expresses itself to an individual during such times and how it deals with the individual in distress reveals a great deal about it.

The family that abandons one of its members in time of distress creates mistrust. If one family member is abandoned, individuals have to wonder who will be next (maybe themselves!). The situation quickly deteriorates to one of "every man for himself."

Privacy

Do family members respect each other's right to privacy within the extended family? In some families it is easy to be overexposed.

More than one family battle has begun because one member intrudes into another's personal business. Many families in business are far too much "in each others' pockets" and need to create privacy.

Well-Defined Boundaries

Do clear lines prevent individuals from getting caught in the middle of conflicts between other family members? One of the most common family business relationship problems occurs when there is a conflict between two family members and one of them involves a third who then gets caught in the middle. Interpersonal boundaries keep this from happening. Healthy boundaries make it possible for individuals "not to take it personally" when someone else gets upset. In other words, they don't take responsibility for another's reactions. This family characteristic is particularly important when the individuals are working together in the business and living together after work!

Summary

This chapter may have offered you something of a new perspective. The systems perspective may change the way you think about the family and its connection with the business. We hope you will find it useful in understanding the complexities of the family business and in sharing that understanding with your clients.

Our purpose in this chapter, as in the others in this book, was not to make family business advisors into family therapists. However, we find that when advisors understand systems and dynamics, they gain insights and can foster problem-solving capabilities within the family business system in addition to addressing specific issues. Before they can do this, though, it's important to assess how the family dynamics affect the business. That is the subject of the next chapter.

Chapter Four

Assessing the Family Business System

One of your tasks in working with a family business is to assess the vitality of the business, the impact that family members have on its viability, and the extent to which the business is managed according to sound business practices. These data should be gathered during one-on-one confidential interviews.

The Assessment Process

In Chapter Two we described how one family advisor held one-on-one confidential interviews with all family members and then a family gathering to present all the issues and observations he had made. This is a practice we recommend. In this chapter we detail the types of data that advisors should try to elicit. We don't mean to imply that separate personal interviews should be held for each category of information. An advisor should gather all types of data about the family and business simultaneously.

When they are interviewed, family members should be told that the information they share will be used only to develop a comprehensive view of the whole system and that nothing they say will be divulged to other family members. The interviews may include non-family-member managers as well as other advisors. The interviews usually consist of a conversation from one to three hours in length. The consultant asks questions, takes notes, and examines relevant documents.

The assessment process may be a formal one in which the consultant goes through a sequence of steps: gathering and analyzing data, preparing a report, and submitting the report to all players often during a family meeting. In other situations, advisors may need to collect data as they go along, making observations and asking questions but not preparing an actual report or having an actual feedback session. (We discuss report preparation and the feedback session at the end of this chapter.)

Most family business advisors prefer the more formal approach because it affords the participants clarity and definition. Because it is more structured and generates more data on a broader range of topics, a formal assessment allows the consultant more flexibility and does a better job of getting the family to look at itself and its issues from a broader perspective. The formal process also allows advisors to bypass some of the usual family rules and blockages and allows information to be gathered more freely.

However, sometimes circumstances preclude a formal assessment. Some families are not comfortable spending the time and money needed to delve into personal and business histories when they have come to an advisor to resolve what seems to them to be a one-dimensional problem. Or the players may live in geographically disparate areas and it would be expensive for them to have the advisor visit each person.

When full-blown interviews are not possible, you still must try to get as much information as possible. But you must be aware that you will have more problems working with the client because you won't have "a full deck of cards." You may want to share this misgiving with clients, explaining that without the full process, you may be limited in effectively designing and implementing necessary interventions. In addition, without a formal assessment you must be prepared for surprises that are sure to emerge.

Purposes of Assessment

There are several important reasons for doing a formal assessment. The assessment helps the advisor gauge what is possible for the business and the family. It provides a set of initial expectations about potential for success in various areas and the data to fill in the outline for your model of the family business system. In general, a formal assessment has three primary objectives:

- To create a forum with the family for inquiry into all the issues related to their situation and to broaden the focus with which the family is willing to explore an issue
- To determine what is relevant for resolving the issues by opening up discussions of subjects that may seem far afield of the problem at hand
- To provide feedback about how to resolve the problems

An additional benefit of a formal assessment is that it gives people an opportunity to speak candidly with the advisor about their thoughts, feelings, and perceptions. This can be very good for them because often they feel that no one has listened to their point of view and that they have the answer to the problem at hand. The advisor gains credibility while some of the individual's frustration is relieved. Also, far more sensitive information may be divulged in a one-on-one interview than in a more public forum.

Assessments also allow the advisor to size up each person. If someone is accessible, friendly, and easy to be with, they are likely to be cooperative. If a person seems mysterious, frightening, or bellicose, the advisor is likely to have a problem getting that person to function as a problem solver with other family members. More difficult but equally important qualities to assess are intelligence and overall degree of emotional maturity. How a person processes information and reacts to what an advisor says is a good indicator of intelligence. Maturity level is often indicated by people's degree of satisfaction with their lives and ability to evaluate their situation with objectivity. An individual's general approach to conflict and conflict resolution is another indication of maturity level. The patterns and themes of an individual's life usually become clear as his or her dynamic in the family does.

Family members' dynamic relationships to their families may be characterized in several ways: they fit in and always fit in, they never fit in, they never felt that the family was supportive, they always felt loved by the family, they always felt that the family should have done something differently than it did, they think they have been a leader in the family.

The *triangulation of data* concept is important in putting together the whole picture. Hearing the same thing from diverse points of view helps increase the validity of the information and identifies gaps or conflicts. Also, when you stop hearing anything new, you can conclude that you have pretty much gotten the picture. Sometimes it is helpful to sit in as a passive observer on family meetings and watch the interactions and dynamics—who speaks, who defers to others, who is in charge, who is silent, and so on.

As you gather data, you will undoubtedly identify issues in the family or the business or both. Often you may sense there's something wrong but be unable to decipher the problems festering beneath the surface. Exhibit 4.1 lists common family business issues and problems and may serve as a guide in putting the pieces of the puzzle together.

The data gathered in the assessment should be related to the model used in working with the family business to address the needs of all stakeholders. Data should be gathered in the areas we describe in the following paragraphs.

The Family's Relationship to the Business

Several issues need to be examined in assessing the relationship of the family to the business.

How the Family Uses the Business

Is the business a birthright, the family heritage, and therefore one that is expected to support them or employ them forever? Is it Dad's baby, while other family members have no desire to be part of it? Is

Exhibit 4.1. Common Family and Business Problems.

Family Dynamic Issues	Family/Business Interface Issues	
Conflict among siblings, other relatives	Entering the business as a family member	Two feuding relatives in the business
Deep feelings of hurt or anger	Active versus passive ownership	Difficulty working with a family member
Lack of trust or respect for in-laws	Family oversight, business involvement	Selling the business
Indirect or lack of communication	Lack of trust in the leader	Diversifying family assets
Indecision about whom to leave estate to	Competence of family business managers	Selecting a successor from many candidates
Disappointment, difficulty with offspring	Distribution of business income	Conflicts between family and non-family employees
Drug or alcohol problem	Divorce of family member in the business	
Career, personal identity confusion		
Family wealth issues		
Conflict between branches of family		

it a drain on the family energy or a source of pride? Understanding how individuals in the family as a whole perceive the business helps advisors to understand behavior and expectations.

Motivation and Competency

Motivation and competency do not always go together. The ideal situation is to have highly motivated, competent family members running the business, but this is not always the case.

Motivation has two components. One is the desire to see the business succeed, the second is the willingness to work hard to achieve that success. Some individuals have this second side and some do not. Sometimes a person is talented but not motivated to work hard. In contrast, a person may put in eighty hours a week but lack skill at running a business.

This point is particularly important if the business is about to be transferred to the younger generation; it is crucial in a larger business or one that is underperforming but has the potential for greater success. Family members often rise to senior leadership positions by birthright rather than through the achievement of milestones on the way to the top. In contrast, professional (nonfamily) managers usually get to where they are based on personal successes at each rung along a ladder that the family member has skipped. The family member may find himself or herself in a position requiring certain skills and abilities that he or she did not have the opportunity to learn. Such individuals cannot go back and gain those opportunities; they require on-the-job training. This is especially true in the interpersonal skill arena. By the time professional managers achieve the presidency of an organization, most of their rough edges have been smoothed; if not, they would not have made it to the top. In contrast, family members who become presidents may not yet have realized their effect on other people. Sometimes consultants spend time coaching a family member president on how to run a company.

An advisor may recommend that in order to make the business more successful, certain people be developed or encouraged to leave. We will see in Chapter Six how families can create support structures to help people develop their capacities and connection to the business.

Compensation and Employment Policies

What kind of lifestyle is the business providing and to how many people? When the company is being transferred to a new generation, a business that was capable of providing a comfortable lifestyle for one family may be called upon to do the same for four; this may not be possible. The compensation policy for family members can tell a great deal about the family's ability to confront such sensitive issues.

Compensation is always a sensitive issue. The most obvious reason is that for most people money has many meanings: it determines their lifestyle and is a reflection of their individual success and self-worth. In a family business, compensation takes on added meaning because it may be considered a measure of comparison between family members with issues of equality involved. Sometimes the amount of compensation becomes intertwined with the degree to which family members feel loved or accepted. Many times this thinking has deep roots, relating back to the degree to which people were satisfied with their early relationships with their parents. It may trigger strong feelings of sibling rivalry, particularly if one sibling earns more than another. The latter may not think it is fair and see this inequality as a replay of earlier injustices.

Because it is such a sensitive issue, most families do not do a very good job at coming up with a rational compensation system. They often confuse the issues of fairness and equality and, rather than pay fair market value for each individual's contribution on the job pay everyone equally. Their sensitivity about compensation prevents them from sorting through ideas, confronting individuals, and developing a system that is workable and that the business can afford.

Families often take one of several paths of least resistance. One is for the father or mother unilaterally to make all the compensation decisions. In this case, there is little awareness within the family about who earns what. The parent's power and intimidation of the child often keeps the potential for conflict under wraps in the short term. Ultimately, however, the compensation issue surfaces because no two jobs are identical and no two people contribute equally. Some families duck the issue by simply paying everyone the same amount. Although they may believe they have solved the fairness problem, they actually have created a larger problem. If three brothers get the same amount of money out of the business, questions are invariably raised about levels of contribution.

The employment policy involves the education, experience, and other criteria required of family members who want to work for the family business. Rarely is the policy explicit. Rather it is usually something that is simply understood. In some family businesses just being a family member satisfies the employment criteria. These families say the business is "here for the family." In larger businesses where such a policy prevails it is typical to find eight members or more working in the business. The potential for conflict in such situations is enormous. At the other end of the spectrum are family businesses that are explicit about the requirements that must be met for employment. An important condition of employment often is the business's explicit need for an individual's talents and skills.

In most cases, entry into a family business is not a rational process but a disjointed one that is sometimes precipitated by an unexpected incident such as death, divorce, or loss of another job.

The family's employment policy is an indication of whether the family is willing to confront sensitive issues or simply reacts emotionally to personal need.

Existence of Legal Documents

Legal documents reduce conflict in times of crisis and facilitate transference of ownership. And, it is hoped, they keep everyone out of the courthouse. Wills and buy-sell agreements should be in place and should reflect appropriate estate and business planning. The impact of the future estate tax burden on successors should also be assessed.

In a smaller business the capabilities of the nonfamily managers and other employees are critical to the current status of the business and what it may achieve in the future. Many times long-term employees have gained seniority through loyalty and the ability to put up with a very difficult situation. They are survivors. Upon close examination it may be that the primary reason these people have achieved longevity is that they can cope with the idiosyncrasies of the founder or the family. Perhaps they are unruffled by high levels of conflict or by autocratic management. Usually these people are trustworthy and honest and have come to represent a sort of extended family to the founder.

If the business needs to change to be more successful then the collective talents and skills of this group are vitally important. An analogy here might be made to members of a sports team. The questions should be the following: How capable are they? What do they bring to the team? How well do they mesh?

The Business's Financial Strengths and Weaknesses

How healthy is the business financially? Reporters and detectives know that to solve a case or a mystery, they need to follow the money. The patterns of how the business generates, keeps track of, and distributes money reveal a lot about the family's attitudes and relationships. The following paragraphs offer some clues to look for to discover the most about the family and the business.

Financial Information

Family businesses vary tremendously in the degree of sophistication of the financial information they generate and use. Some business owners meet once a year in April with their accountants to sign the company tax returns. Other families are sensitive about sharing financial information with people with whom they are not familiar or have had little experience. Many business owners don't even like to share financial information with other family members, even those who own stock in the company, or with members of the senior management team, even those who are part of the family. If this is the case then the advisor should negotiate as much access as possible.

In all cases, financial data become an essential part of the data collected. Any financial information available helps give an idea of the financial strength of the business and how successful it is.

Attitude Toward Debt

It is interesting how many family businesses eschew debt. Professional managers may wince at this underutilization of capital but this kind of conservative approach to risk can pay off in difficult times. A business that seems to have more debt than is appropriate may find its viability vulnerable to economic and market fluctuations. A family's level of awareness about its potential to repay outstanding debt and its motivation and discipline to do so may reveal its degree of business sophistication and knowledge of the business. Some family businesses pile up loans with little or no sense of an amortization schedule for repayment.

Revenue and Profit

The profitability of the business can be revealing from several standpoints. A decline in gross margins over the years may reflect a management problem, such as unrealistic pricing or an inability to track and manage costs and efficiencies. It is important, however, to find out how competitors are doing in order to determine the extent to which industry conditions are affecting margins.

Family businesses also fluctuate in their profitability. Mack Trapp, an estate planning and tax professional and the past president of the American College of Trust and Estate Counsel (ACTEC), suggests that the reason most family businesses are reluctant to share financial information is because they are less profitable than many public companies. It seems strange but many family businesses seem either to scrape by at low profitability for many years or to be consistently profitable. Others seem to be at the mercy of market conditions and are enormously profitable some years and lose money in others. Most family businesses demonstrate a remarkable tenacity and manage to survive.

Often the profitability of the business reflects the owners' expectations and perceptions about success. If they have modest expectations these can become self-fulfilling prophecies and the business is in fact only moderately successful. But if the family will not accept anything less than strong profits, some way is usually found to produce them. Although the industry the business is in also affects profit expectations, in the end it comes down to the attitude of the owners.

In many service firms the industry average before-tax profit is between 15 percent and 20 percent; in the printing industry the average is 4 percent. A number of printing companies are family-owned or owner-managed businesses. For a printing business to achieve a 10 percent profit margin it has to do something very different from its peers. It is easy for a family to have modest expectations in the face of this industry average. In recognition of this fact, the printing trade association has published ten things that more successful printing companies do differently. So greater success *is* possible.

How the Family Measures Business Health

Rarely do members of a family-owned business calculate such standard big-business measurements as return on investment or return on equity. If inactive family shareholders do raise the question, active owners or managers may dodge the issue by pointing out other dimensions of a satisfactory investment. If things are going well, shareholders may be happy enough to take their distributions and not probe further. However, the rate of return can become an important issue to dissatisfied minority shareholders.

This may produce conflict in that it brings into play a difference in values for the dissatisfied person from the rest of the family. The issue is not usually easily resolved because the business cannot

restructure itself to produce such information easily. It is also difficult to resolve because if people wish to opt out of a business, it is
hard to return their investment to them.

Probably the most important piece of financial information is
the cash flow statement. The cash flow statement reflects the ability of the business to generate cash and satisfy balance sheet requirements. Cash flow information should be assessed against how much
money the owners are taking out of the business.

Perks

In assessing profitability, the profit reported on the profit and loss
statement should be adjusted for such "owner beneficial expenses"
as cars, bonuses, and so on. Once these have been added back in, a
more accurate picture is achieved. If the profit percentage is low
and the family is not taking much out of the business, a family advisor might press to make the business more successful to compensate
the family members for the hard work they are doing and the risk
they are taking. After all, one of the reasons for putting up with all
of the headaches of running a business is the potential for significant financial reward.

Any balanced assessment requires that the value of perks and
the salary paid to the family be compared with fair market compensation. If the family's perks exceed fair market then the amount
by which they exceed it must be added back into the profits to get
a fair profile of the business performance.

Facility Maintenance

The condition of the plant and equipment is very important when
the issue of succession comes up. If adequate attention has not been
paid to upkeep of the physical plant, there is a real challenge to the
future success of the business. Large amounts of capital will be
needed to replenish the plant and equipment. If that capital is not

available then the business's long-term success may be in jeopardy. A previously successful business can very quickly decline because of lack of attention.

Assessing the physical status of a business is relatively easy. Stores, offices, and plants are either new or old. They are either well maintained or run down. They are either clean or dirty. Advisors should compare the business with industry norms for age and condition of equipment. The issue is whether the family has continued to invest the capital required to keep the company vital. Sometimes the family pulls money out of the business instead of making this investment. Or a company that is not generating much profit may simply put off investing because the money is not there. In some cases, even when funds are available, a founder who is getting on in years has little motivation for continued investment because his need to invest in his own future is reduced.

Business Strategy, Structure, and Management

A complete assessment includes the family's relationship to the business, the financial strengths and weaknesses of the business, and the business itself—especially its strategy, operating structure, and management team. These can be gauged by assessing aspects of the business described in the following paragraphs.

Vitality of Products and Markets

Businesses operate within industries. All industries experience cycles. It is important to determine the current point in the industry's cycle in order to project the long-term potential of the company's products and markets. Is the potential for growth or decline? If the company's market includes only one or two major customers who have personal ties to the family business founder then once those customers or the business founder retires the ties may be severed and the market potential dramatically changed. If the business cycle is reaching a point where new product development and innovation are required, then the advisor must assess whether the business is capable of meeting the challenge.

Advisors also need to factor in the key decision makers' knowledge, awareness, and sensitivity to these issues. For instance, let us suppose that a business owner's interest and involvement in the business plateaus just as the business requires rejuvenation. The pivotal success of the business may have occurred fifteen or twenty years earlier and the business may have been riding out a market wave that is about to crest.

Use of Planning Tools

We believe that family businesses that use planning tools (strategic, operational, and business planning tools) see better results on the bottom line. It is important to look for and encourage strategic thinking and planning. With such practices the business looks realistically at what it must do in the future. This is especially critical in times of fast change in the business environment.

Although owners of independent, privately owned companies often don't see the need for such systems, the owners will have a hard time fine-tuning operations, delegating authority and responsibility, and creating feedback systems to employees about how the system is doing without them. It is also hard to evaluate the impact of business decisions when there is no established method for measuring the outcome.

The Senior Management Team

In many family businesses, a person rises to the top because of loyalty and good survival skills. But when turnover is low and managers long-lived, the business may not benefit from infusions of new blood. The bottom line is that a business is only as good as the senior management team is and this includes their ability to solve problems, to foster a new vision, and to make critical decisions.

Profit Orientation   HENRY HARDER

In businesses that are not profit oriented, resources are not properly aligned. The advisor must assess the margins the business is able to generate; these reflect its capability to be profitable.

What the Family Does with Its Money

How much does the family reinvest? How much do they take out? Either extreme—taking out too much or too little—merits an evaluation.

Presenting the Assessment to the Family

When you have amassed all the data, analyze the various dimensions of the family, the individuals, and the business. After this analysis, most family business consultants prepare a written report. One approach is first to give an overall assessment of the current status, detailing those factors that bode well for success in the future and those that give rise to concern. A second section of the report outlines the general goal areas for the family to pursue. Finally, a third lists specific steps and recommendations.

A written report should be presented during a face-to-face session. This feedback session provides a "readiness check" of the family's willingness to make changes. If you feel confident about your findings but the family is very resistant, this says a lot about what you can hope to achieve. In contrast, if the feedback session goes well it may offer the opportunity to refine the report and begin to form it into a game plan for moving forward. It is important to clarify different perceptions and get everyone's perceptions in harmony with those of the others.

It is important that more than just one or two family owners or managers be present at this session. You must ask that all the owners, or the whole family, be present, because your report concerns everyone and they will all have to work together to ensure the business's good health.

There is one caveat, however. Your findings are observations; your suggestions are based on hypotheses. You should encourage the family to challenge, question, and talk with you. Family members may misunderstand some of your points. Indeed, one of your findings may actually be wrong or reflect a limited perspective. Therefore it makes all the more sense to present an assessment tentatively and with a great deal of discussion before both you and the family accept it.

As noted a few paragraphs earlier, the feedback session can serve as a jumping-off point for formulating a development plan. In the next chapters we will help you weigh the severity of the problems as well as your own expertise and comfort in dealing with them, in order to select an appropriate level of your involvement and responsibility in the solution plan.

Summary

In this chapter we described some tools for assessing the ways in which families and their businesses interact. We presented the kinds of information that advisors need to gather when they are dealing with a family business. In addition, we suggested that they explore some nontraditional methods to bring what they learned back to the family. In the next chapter we take a look at the tools and methods to use to put process consulting to work.

Part Two

Tools and Techniques

The chapters in Part Two describe some of the tools and techniques that advisors can use to gain a broader perspective on family businesses and become more effective in resolving conflict. Chapter Five presents an overview of process consulting tools for intervening in a family business. It focuses on setting up a family work session and helping the family talk about and consider how it works and how it can improve its effectiveness. Chapter Six examines the most difficult family conflicts a professional may need to handle. It offers mediation and process consultation tools that can be used to help families deal with their conflicts. A special section is devoted to situations resulting from substance abuse. In Chapter Seven we discuss boundaries and the structures and policies a family must develop in order to manage effectively both the business of the business and the business of the family.

Chapter Five

Developing Effective Interventions

Once you have gathered data about the family, the individuals within it, and their business, you are ready to use your knowledge and insights to develop interventions.

An intervention is a planned interaction with a client in which the consultant presents or brings to the surface the data for discussion and then develops together with the client a range of alternatives for resolving conflicts, building an effective family and business team, integrating the various clusters of stakeholders, or changing business practices and processes. The approach taken by expert advisors and by process consultants differs somewhat. An expert advisor studies the situation, writes a report, and recommends actions relating to issues within her specific area of expertise. A process consultant works with the client to develop a plan focusing on his area of expertise as well as on any other interpersonal and business issues that, if unresolved, may prevent successful resolution of the problem at hand. The criteria presented in Table 2.1 in Chapter Two can help you consider which role may be appropriate for you.

Who Is Involved in Each Step?

The number of family members to involve in an intervention is a question for the advisor and the family to decide. The whole family may be included or only those working or having ownership in the business. However, although the family often tries to limit the number of participants, we have often found it important to broaden the list. More people may have an interest in the outcome than may at first be apparent. For example, although many families are reluctant to include spouses in the deliberations, spouses are critical observers of the family and have an influence and a stake in the outcome. Rather than allow them to get their information from one person alone—their spouse—we suggest they be a part of any gatherings where the family's future is decided.

When advisors work with an individual the two generally communicate directly and can clarify points and focus matters. But when working with a family, if the advisor's interface is with only one individual his message is subjected to that individual's interpretation and communication skills. His precise concerns may not be transmitted to everyone or they may not be transmitted correctly. If the individual doesn't fully understand the matter or doesn't completely understand how it relates to other family members there is potential for a real problem.

As a matter of course, the advisor needs to ask, "Who are the stakeholders in this matter and how will they be informed and kept abreast of details pertaining to it?" Once the stakeholder group has been identified it is preferable to communicate with them all directly as a group. Doing this may mean challenging some of the ways the family usually does things. If some individuals in the family are threatened by the idea of a group meeting, it may be more effective to communicate at first in writing. In this case, each group member should receive the same materials. Because some individuals may not be open listeners or active participants, it may also be advisable to ask each group member to write down his or her individual concerns about the family business and then have all read what the others have written. In this way, any misunderstandings are resolved at the outset. Once they learn this process, some families adopt it as a routine procedure to prevent future misunderstandings.

It is wise never to disregard or dismiss any individual's need to know. You may have to tell the business owner or patriarch that informing people is not the same as giving them decision power.

They can be informed even if they are not decision makers. Stakeholders (including those in the family and in the business and outside professional advisors) should be included as frequently as possible in meetings to promote full information flow. Getting the accountant, banker, financial planner, and other advisors together is sometimes quite helpful.

At each step of the intervention, you may have to explain very carefully what you are doing and why it is important. This kind of up-front explanation is time well spent because it diminishes misunderstandings later on.

Which Problems Are Addressed First?

A family business consultant moves the group incrementally past a series of goals. The successful accomplishment of each becomes the foundation for the next. The process should move from the simple to the complex, from the easy to the difficult.

Figure 5.1 illustrates how several interventions may be necessary to move the family business from frustration, conflict, and ineffective practices to a successful resolution. Each arrow represents an intervention.

One arrow may be the development of a new marketing plan. The second may represent working with two brothers who don't get along. The third may represent developing senior managers with

Figure 5.1. One Intervention per Problem.

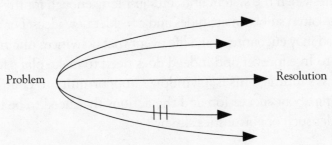

better team-building experience. The fourth may refer to individual work with Dad, who is having trouble letting go of the business.

The arrow that appears to be blocked by crosshatches represents the inevitable situation in which one of the interventions "gets stuck." The group may be inclined to focus all its energy on the lack of success of this one effort and not track the progress of the others. If the resistance to one direction is strong, the best approach may be to set aside this effort for the time being. The problem should be put on hold until the individuals' abilities to work together as a group are strengthened. For example, Dad's inability to transfer control should not hamper the development of a marketing plan. If the group members learn to work together on a less difficult challenge and experience successful communication and resolution of it they may be better able to confront the more difficult issues in a more relaxed manner.

As the figure indicates, at any point in time an advisor may work on multiple agendas within the various systems. Some of these agendas affect single individuals or systems and others are interlocked among several individuals and systems. For example, at the same time an advisor may be helping two brothers who have never gotten along find new ways of working together, increasing the self-esteem of a sister so she can become a viable player, working with the father in succession planning, and trying to develop a more positive mood in the group as a whole to overcome a recent negative emotional event. The key to accomplishing multiple agendas is to be alert for opportunities or windows for change. These windows are times when the system unfreezes just long enough for the members to soften stubborn attitudes and consider new ideas. For example, Dad may encounter some life event that convinces him he isn't going to live forever and indeed does need to make plans for the business's future. This is a window of opportunity to change his thinking about succession and the actions that need to be taken. Don't let such opportunities slip by!

Offering Choices and Options

Somewhere along the line we all got programmed to give "the right answer." But when advisors work with a family, it isn't long before they learn that being right and being correct are not always the same. An advisor may have the correct answer to a set of presenting conditions only to have the family reject it out of hand. If this happens, it may be a clue that there is an emotional or psychological blockage standing in the way. In consulting, "right" and "correct" are nebulous concepts. A successful intervention requires presenting alternatives and options that emerge from the information the advisor has collected and developed together with the family members. Further, the advisor should recognize that when one person demands the perfect solution, this individual has personal issues that may make him or her difficult to work with.

Earlier we mentioned that doing nothing is always an option. Although rarely a feasible option, offering it as an alternative to consider and exploring the consequences can be a useful exercise. Quitting is another option that an advisor may need to consider in some cases.

An Off-Site Family Work Session

A work session or retreat that lasts two or three days can be a useful vehicle for beginning the planning process and setting the stage for the family to work together as a team. For many families such an occasion represents the first time they come together to talk systematically about family and business issues. Of course, individuals will react to the suggestion of a family work session with concern, excitement, questions, and perhaps apprehension, depending on the situation.

The main goal of a family work session is to take the family from where it is in its individual, family, and business life stages and move it as close to its optimal goal as possible. This movement must be orchestrated in a low-key and nonthreatening manner. If the previously accomplished assessment has determined that the family business system is fragile and the individuals highly polarized, the design must be very controlled, the focus and specific tasks explicit, and the structure and process clearly articulated in advance.

Advance Planning

The first step necessary in planning this kind of retreat is to get the commitment of the whole group and then appoint a subcommittee as a planning group to work on its design. The subcommittee members and their advance work contain the seeds of success or failure. The planning group should be composed of a cross section of family members including both men and women and including people who are verbal and people who are not, people who are designated leaders and people who are not generally in a leadership position, and so on. A planning group of this type is needed because some of the family business work will get done during the planning process simply through the discussions that take place. Furthermore, if handled correctly, the family retreat will already contain a subgroup of converted advocates who understand the issues and may even have a unified view on matters.

The date of the first retreat should be set far enough in advance to allow people to incorporate it into their schedules but soon enough to seem imminent.

Who Should Facilitate the Session?

The advisor's purpose in the first work session is to submit the oral or written report of the initial assessment; establish shared goals within the family; begin to establish structures and processes that enable the family to deal with issues that involve both the family and the business; and strengthen the capabilities of family members to relate constructively.

It is important that a third-party facilitator run the retreat in order to minimize any distortions in the desired group processes caused by family dynamics or particular role definitions. Should that facilitator be you? It depends on the family situation, your experience level, and your comfort with the presenting issues and problems you have uncovered during the assessment process. If the client's problem has been identified at level A or B (see again Table 2.1 in Chapter Two) almost any professional should be able to facilitate a family work session. Probably only advisors who feel confident in their ability to use process consulting skills should facilitate a session for clients with problems at level C. In some cases, the client may best be served by bringing in a specialist in communication, problem solving, and mediation.

Who Should Attend the Session?

The participants involved vary from family to family. The first work session usually includes only family members involved in the business or lineal descendants of the founder and their spouses. Including only this select group makes the most sense in very polarized families because it gives the advisor a chance to defuse tension and work out some initial hurdles. Deep conflicts usually stem from early family difficulties and require some privacy and security to come out. The fundamental premise is not to establish a mechanism that may ultimate create barriers between the fundamental family unit of husband and wife. When families insist that members keep secrets from their spouses, they are setting up those spouses to feel alienated. This is not to say that spouses should always be allowed to vote on issues pertaining to business operations. However, they should attend meetings in order to be fully informed about issues in which they have a stake.

Children are usually not included in the early work sessions. The adults simply do not need the distraction. Children of age fourteen or so can be included at later sessions. A specific program should be designed to get the teenagers up to speed on what the family business is all about. This especially applies to the issue of confidentiality around family business system matters discussed at the work session.

However, if there is no severe conflict, getting the entire family together at a retreat is positive because it promotes family cohesiveness and good times.

The Course of the Session

A typical family retreat begins on a Friday evening and runs through Sunday afternoon. The first gathering of the weekend should be designed to assure a successful outcome. By the end of it, the participants should have obtained some new data, gained a clear picture of the mechanics and agenda of the weekend to come, and been encouraged or required to interact with each other in some manner. An effective first exercise is to ask participants to write on a five-by-eight-inch card the answers to some questions that they will share with the others. Two examples are the following: (1) In your opinion, what will be the best outcomes from this work session for the extended family, for the business, and for you individually? (2) What special concerns do you have about this work session? With groups of more than a dozen, everyone may be asked to stand up, mill about, and in a period of some fifteen minutes pair off with at least four people separately to share and discuss what they have written on their cards. Smaller groups may be handled in this way or in the group as a whole.

This exercise forces people to think about why they are at the retreat and what they want from the time and money they have invested in it. It encourages them to think about several elements: family, business, and self. And they have to share publicly, which itself becomes a kind of commitment. The exercise also encourages verbal interaction, often between parties who do not regularly interact. The physical process of standing and milling about "mixes things" and breaks from the static pattern of people coming into a room and sitting in affinity groups. The advisor should take every opportunity during work sessions to form groups, mixing them so that family members are forced to interact in different combinations.

The Location

An off-site location is best because it is neutral territory and also less given to interruptions. A facility with a catering or convention department that is flexible and can accommodate the needs of work sessions is best. Ideally, the facility will offer formal and informal restaurants, recreational facilities, and a private meeting room large enough for round tables that seat six to eight people and for milling-around space.

The Agenda

The pace of the retreat should be guided by the family work ethic. The agenda should include a mix of business items, family communication and team-building exercises, opportunities for individuals to share events in their personal lives, opportunities to express thoughts about the family and the business, and a group exercise to explore the challenges of moving forward. The agenda should push for clear outcomes and understandings.

Playtime should be planned into the design. Play can range from family skits, a talent show, and a golf tournament to a family Olympics. A party, usually scheduled for the last night, can be planned by volunteers after the last afternoon's session. The facilitator should meet with the volunteers and give them a box containing party supplies with instructions as follows: "In this box are the makings of a party. Please set up the room to have a good time."

A Sample Family Work Session Agenda

The sample agenda shown in Exhibit 5.1 incorporates all the design issues discussed in the previous paragraphs. It should be noted that sessions are never longer than three hours and usually include two topics. There is always some movement built in to give people an opportunity to change groups. It is imperative to send an agenda to all family members in advance of the retreat with an offer to answer questions they may have. This can help reduce any anxiety family members may have about the session.

Communication-Building Exercises

Every work session has several common elements, which are conducted under the guidance of the advisor or an outside facilitator.

Reconnecting. Early in the work session, the facilitator should allow each participant to be given the undivided attention of the entire group and take a minute and a half to three minutes to talk about what he or she has been doing and what he or she is concerned about. This little talk may be about the individual's personal life, the family, or the business. At one such reconnecting exercise, one participant said she was so uncomfortable with the family and her role in it that there was nothing she felt comfortable talking about. Everyone sat silently during her allotted time. Later, some family members were so concerned that they followed up and asked her about it. The power of this simple technique is that it gives everyone equal time instead of allowing only the most verbal members to set the agenda. Even silence can communicate a deep concern that other members will be unlikely to ignore.

The family can hold a reconnecting session every time they get together.

Exhibit 5.1. Family Work Session Agenda.

Thursday:

Dinner (prior to the start of Work Session I)

7:00–9:00 P.M. Work Session I

Review of Agenda

"Best Outcomes" Exercise

Feedback presentation by facilitator: "How I understand your family and
  your business"

Friday:

8:00–8:30 A.M. Continental breakfast

8:30–11:30 A.M. Work Session II

The new archetype: Helping the family see itself in a different light, in
  family and individual life stages

Communications and problem-solving exercises

Mini-lecture about boundaries

11:30 A.M.–1:30 P.M. Lunch break

1:30–4:00 P.M. Work Session III

Understanding who we are:
  • Define the norms and values that will serve us in the future.
  • Identify the norms and values we will leave behind.
  • Build trust: Given the disappointments and misunderstandings of the
    past, what actions and paths can we take to build trust?

Our lifeline and the photos of a lifetime: Members were asked to bring
three or four of their favorite photos from their family albums. These are
placed on a long strip of butcher paper that contains a continuum with
dates. Members retell family stories and begin to see how the family looks
at itself, as this is revealed in the photos they have chosen.

Building family shields: Members form into teams and are given art materials with which they are asked to create a family crest. This abstract foundation allows people to project how they feel about the family.

4:00–7:00 P.M. Dinner break

7:00–9:00 P.M. Work Session IV

Our community, our business: Past, present, future
  • Business events on the lifeline—how they affect the community
  • Recent ten years
  • The past as a window to the future—our community impact

Exhibit 5.1. Family Work Session Agenda *(continued)*.

Saturday: Communications about the business

8:00 –8:30 A.M. Continental breakfast

8:30–11:30 A.M. Work Session V

The business:
- Who owns what?
- Trusts, boards, executives, governance
- Communication and advice from family to the business
- Reviewing business practices

Ownership: Entry and exit procedures: Impact of an owner exit on the business

11:30 A.M.–12:45 P.M. Lunch break

12:45–1:30 P.M. Open time

1:30–4:00 P.M. Work Session VI

Defining the purpose of the businesses:
- Creating the vehicle to achieve the purpose: Who in the family will participate?
- What's in it for me? What's in it for us?

4:00–6:00 P.M. Break

6:00 P.M. until . . . A celebration of family: An evening of fun with your rellies

Sunday: Attending to the business of the family

8:00–8:30 A.M. Continental breakfast

8:30–11:00 A.M. Work Session VII

Fantasy letter: Everyone writes what the year 2000 will be like. Then they make a composite of the themes and work backward year by year to figure out what must be done to achieve that, creating a future mindset, tapping into dreams of the future, and suggesting ways to help implement them.

Preparing a follow-up plan:

11:00 A.M.–1:00 P.M. Lunch break

1:00–4:00 P.M. Work Session VIII

Review of the 10 qualities of families that stay positively connected and in business:
- Define "shared activities" for maintenance of relationships.
- What are the things we as a family want to leave behind?
- What must we do to continue what we have developed here?

Appreciating circles

Last words

4:00 P.M. Adjournment

Paraphrasing. How do we know if someone has really heard us? When someone says, "I understand," what exactly did he or she understand? Have you ever wondered why voices get louder and points of view get restated over and over during a heated discussion?

Having confidence that one's message was received as intended is a rare experience. The odds are against our understanding one another unless we really work at it. A number of barriers interfere with understanding.

1.   *Assumptions about the end of the story.* A common listening error is to hear the first part of a statement and assume we know the rest. Rather than patiently listening to the whole story, we interrupt and interject our own perspectives, often missing an important point and rudely implying that our perspective is more important than the speaker's.

2.   *Words as symbols for images, ideas, or objects.* Our use of words may conjure up a picture in a listener's mind that is different from the one we have in mind. For example, in some restaurants meat ordered medium rare looks as if it was just ripped from the beast; at others, it has a gray-brown coloring and not even a faint sign of pink. We often falsely assume that others' minds hold the same image as ours.

3.   *Internal and external distractions.* We are all susceptible to distractions from the speaker, such as noises or activity in our immediate environment. Emotional reactions to the speaker, thoughts trailing off in our minds, and even growling stomachs also cause us to lose track of the speaker's words. Internal and external distractions contribute to our missing important aspects of a message so that we are left with a false or incomplete understanding.

With all the inevitable barriers to communication, it is rarely safe to assume people fully and accurately understand a speaker. Facilitators can teach family members an effective tool to enhance listening skills and understanding: paraphrasing, simply confirming one's understanding with a reflective response. After hearing someone complete a statement, the advisor can tell listeners to repeat back their understanding of the message, in order to confirm that they have accurately heard it, before adding their own response. When we paraphrase we do the following:

- Let the speaker know we are interested in understanding her perspective
- Verify that our understanding is correct or gain the opportunity to revise it if we have misunderstood
- Let the speaker know her message has been received and that she can stop pressing her perspective and be more open to ours (reducing defensiveness and building trust)
- Demonstrate our understanding rather than merely claim we understand

Typical paraphrases begin with the following expressions: "So what you are saying is. . . ." "If I understand you correctly. . . ." "In other words. . . ." "To summarize, then. . . ." "Let me check my understanding. . . ."

Most of us pay closer attention to a teacher when we know we will be tested; when we paraphrase in essence we are testing ourselves.

Listening Skill Enhancement.   Most people respond halfway through another person's expression. We tend to stop listening in the middle and formulate our thoughts. Often, however, the true message—the point or feeling the person is trying to express—gets stated later. The listening skill enhancer exercise gets listeners to find the "pearl" in the other's expression.

The advisor divides attendees into groups of three, with one person designated A (the speaker), another B (the listener), and the third C (the observer). This exercise is repeated three times so that each person has an opportunity to experience each role. The speaker is then given five minutes to talk while the listener periodically paraphrases the speaker's statements and tries to interpret the speaker's feelings. At the end of the five minutes, the observer takes one minute to give feedback to the listener regarding the accuracy and manner of paraphrasing. When the feedback is finished, the speaker and listener interact for another two minutes so the listener can try to use the feedback received. When the time is up, the round ends and the three change roles. Someone can take notes, creating a chart like that shown in Table 5.1.

The importance of humor should not be forgotten. An example comes from a family that had just begun to hold quarterly meetings. Frank, the business founder, was a real talker. Once started, he was hard to stop. One of his sons brought an antique soap box and a kitchen timer to a meeting. Frank was told to stand on the soap box with the timer ticking as he gave his reports. When families can learn to laugh at themselves as Frank did there is easier resolution of many matters that vex families in business.

Similarly, some time should be built in for family fun. One of the purposes of the retreat is for the family to begin to experience and enjoy each other as individuals. Many families need to learn that having fun together is just as important as working together. Doing something fun also breaks up a long day.

Primary Tasks of the Family Work Session

In the following sections we outline the main goals for a family work session.

Table 5.1. Listening Skill Enhancement Exercise.

Role	Round One	Round Two	Round Three
Speaker	A	C	B
Listener	B	A	C
Observer	C	B	A

Clarify the Family's Core Values and Purposes

A consultant needs to establish a positive basis for work so that the family gains confidence in dealing with difficult issues and conflicts. If the family has come to you because they feel "stuck," they probably have made a number of ineffective attempts to work out their problems and make decisions. Some families may even be in a state of despair and fear they will never find a solution to their problems. It is particularly important that the initial interventions are an attempt to reverse such negativism and establish a foundation for positive and rewarding experiences for going forward. One way to turn the situation around is to engage the family in an exercise of recounting positive stories about the family over the years. These stories promote positive memories and values and themes usually emerge. In turn, the experiences can become the foundation for a family mission statement.

Much like a corporate mission statement, the family mission statement should address the family's future direction, its desires for the family as a whole and the individuals within it, and the values it stands for. The statement usually reflects the values under which the family wants to conduct itself and its expectations for its members. The process of developing a family mission statement tends to promote good feelings and gets people in touch with things they feel good about and can be proud of. It also may help people realize that although they have some problems they also have a lot of positive attributes.

Developing a family mission statement requires little technical expertise so it is also an opportunity to empower family members who have been previously disenfranchised. By giving them an important role to play and bringing all individuals more completely into the process, the entire group's self-esteem can rise.

Plan for Business Success

A critical goal of the retreat is to get the family to focus on the success of the business. Many times the family is so absorbed with its own internal problems and dynamics that it doesn't focus on the business. Also, many family businesses are characterized by informal practices that inhibit growth and success. The family should be urged to establish professional management practices and a talented management team. They should be coached to focus on the bottom line and not tolerate low returns on equity. We use the term "coach" because some families really are not profit oriented and have a nonchalant attitude toward their business's success. Such businesses are usually underperforming if successful at all. Putting the emphasis on profit helps align resources and expectations in any business.

Ideally, the family should adopt a planning process that begins with the development of an overall vision of the family and business future; a business mission statement; and a strategic plan and a business plan for the coming year. Subsequently, the family should regularly monitor progress on these plans, creating an ongoing process that starts at the beginning of each fiscal year. As a business expands and nonfamily members occupy key positions, they must be included in the process.

This planning process achieves a number of important objectives:

- It communicates to all the stakeholders the direction of the business and what it is trying to achieve.
- It provides a vehicle for holding family employees accountable for their performance.
- It promotes good management in the company and may be used to encourage delegation of authority and responsibility.
- It may serve as a basis for a compensation system based upon performance and merit.
- It is a good way to make the business successful.

Developing a systematic business plan that forges a new direction is one of the most important activities an advisor can

undertake, especially if there is a lot of confusion about the state of
the business and frustration with its limited success. It provides a
focus that also helps the family develop more objective problem-
solving and decision-making skills in the business that they can
learn to transfer to emotional and interpersonal issues. Usually
developing a plan is a positive experience that helps family members feel in better control of their world.

Once family business members begin to iron out some of their
most difficult business and family issues, nonfamily managers may
be invited to future family work sessions.

Business planning involves the development of forecasts and
budgets for each division, a long-range plan and a plan for the coming year. Each senior manager becomes responsible for accomplishing a discrete segment of the plan. In the process, roles and
responsibilities are clarified. If successful, this kind of business planning can shift the family dynamic from one of continuous conflict,
informal communication and confusion to systematic discussions
and business solutions. Putting formal business plans in action
enable the family business to establish professional systems that will
enhance governance, education, and dissemination of information.
(These issues are explained in more detail in Chapter Seven.)

Present the State-of-the-Business Report

The first retreat offers an opportunity to review overall financial
performance and discuss new products and directions as well as
challenges of the marketplace. This activity should be updated periodically at future family work sessions or family forum meetings (see
Chapter Six).

The business review sessions at the retreats emphasize owner
responsibility, financial principles, and general business concepts.
They do not include discussion of day-to-day operations. By attending these sessions, younger family members begin to learn how to
handle confidential matters. Everyone in the family learns about

and is proud of the business they own. There is a time limit—usually not more than one hour—and a printed agenda.

Develop Mediating Structures

Creation of a family forum, family board, or board of directors and advisory board is important. These are legitimate ways for stakeholders to remain informed and involved in the business. (See Chapter Seven.)

Develop Conflict Resolution Mechanisms

As we have already discussed, when working with a family business it is often necessary not only to help the family resolve current issues and challenges but also to build capability to face future issues. You will have a difficult time initiating a process of clarification and relationship building if a family can't constructively confront sensitive and emotional issues. Many families are not skilled at conflict resolution. They draw upon models developed in childhood and usually either repress concerns or explode. In Chapter Six we review constructive and destructive family conflict and recommend how advisors can effectively help family business clients work through conflict.

Develop Win-Win Solutions for Everyone

When one family member always seeks to prevail, the big loser is the entire family. If interactions between family members are primarily win-lose there will ultimately be angry family members who don't want to continue to play.

The Japanese understand the importance of "saving face." They will discuss a matter for as long as it takes to reach a position where there was no loss of face for any of the parties to the transaction. Fundamentally, such a position requires sharing power. With a win-

win approach, all parties to a transaction feel that they share in the beneficial outcome. The emphasis is on the word *feel*. If people feel they have lost or were overpowered in a transaction, the details make little difference.

The win-win approach stems from game theory. In any game, the possible outcomes are win-win, win-lose, and lose-lose. If a person enters a transaction with a win-win strategy, then it is a possible outcome; it can shift down to win-lose or to lose-lose. However, if the opening strategy is win-lose, there are only two outcomes: win-lose and lose-lose. In theory and reality, when a party elects a win-lose strategy only rarely does it ascend to a win-win outcome.

The fundamental principle is helping people articulate a solution that will serve the interests of the entire group. Only when that has been articulated can it be used as a criteria. What will the future look like if everybody is content? "I'd have an interesting job." "I'd have an opportunity to have influence." "We'd have amicable relationships." All such visions can get translated into current activities that will lead to these outcomes.

Reframe, Explore, "Wonder"

One of the key tools in the consultant's kit is to help the family see a situation in a new light. This is called *reframing*. For example, if a brother and sister have always fought and they bring this family behavior into their work together in the family business, the advisor might observe how each one brings the strength of a different perspective into the business and point out how the business would suffer if either perspective was lost. Doing this reframes their conflict as a necessary dynamic to the growth of the business.

Another form of reframing is making connections between past and present behavior. The assessment process described in Chapter Three, in particular creating a family genogram, should help advisors discover connections between past and present behaviors. Sometimes when a challenge is put into the context of its evolution from old issues, an advisor can help a family release itself from a pattern that is no longer working for them.

For example, Cullen, a seventy-five-year-old second-generation owner, not only refused to retire or set a date for future retirement but also would not relinquish an ounce of control to his sons, aged forty-five and fifty. The two could not see past their frustration. The advisor noted that the grandfather, who had died in the saddle four years earlier at age ninety-three, had also kept a tight grasp on the reins. Indeed, Sam had only begun to enjoy responsibility and authority at age seventy-one and he wasn't ready to relinquish it. When the family saw the problem in this historical context, they were able to realize that they didn't have to repeat this pattern. They began to respect one another's need for some control and were able to see, discuss, and consider other options.

It is not uncommon for the client to expect the advisor to have the definitive answer. However, a mature, experienced advisor has the knowledge and skill to "wonder" and explore with the client before coming to a conclusion. When you think you see a pattern, rather than pronouncing "We have a pattern here" it is preferable to suggest there may be a pattern. The pronouncement style of response may push a client into a box that he does not want to be in and lead to resentment or anger against the person who put him there. The technique of "wondering" or exploring the possibility of something is a gentler way of getting the client to look at a touchy issue.

Follow-Up Meetings

Quarterly meetings are excellent vehicles through which to communicate. We wish that every business would have them with clockwork regularity. When families ignore the importance of regular communication they set themselves up for a crisis.

In most cases family work sessions are positive experiences that the family will want to repeat on a regular basis. Usually during the course of the first retreat, a number of issues that require follow-up tasks arise. This "to do" list, along with notes of the retreat taken from the flip charts containing key points made in the session, should be transcribed and distributed to everyone. This lends credibility to the event and jogs foggy memories about what they discussed and decided.

Summary

In this chapter we presented strategies and techniques for bringing families together to begin change. We discussed ways to build communication, select targets for intervention, and create family work sessions. The fruits of success in these activities are stronger, more effectively managed, and more profitable businesses. Higher levels of professionalism in business operation leads to greater satisfaction among the family and the family owners.

In the next chapter we look at how to deal with deeper and more serious types of family conflict.

Chapter Six

Helping Families in Conflict

For most advisors, one of the most intimidating aspects of working with a family business is the high level of conflict they may be forced to deal with. This chapter provides an understanding of the different types of conflict, explains roles that different types of advisors—including experts, family systems-informed experts, and process consultants—can take to deal with it, and describes tools they can use to prevent and cope with it.

Let us begin with an example. Attorney John Griffin had spent close to a hundred hours working with Samuel, the founder of a commercial construction and development firm, developing a beautifully constructed estate plan. The tax savings were significant, the buy-sell provisions would secure ownership of the business within the family, and thanks to collaboration with insurance specialists and the family accountant it was assured that Sam's wife, Helen, would be well provided for if Sam died before she did. There was only one problem: Sam hadn't signed the will or discussed the plan with his children. He was afraid that when he did conflict among the children would blow up the business.

Sam was uncomfortable openly discussing the future, his own death, and the succession of the ownership and management of the business. He was even more fearful of the jealousy and bickering he expected among his kids. Tony, his oldest son and an aggressive personality, had always believed that he should be in charge. The other children were intimidated by him. Rita, Sam and Helen's daughter, did not work in the business but served on the board and represented

109

the family in the community. Skip, their youngest child, was hard-working and conscientious and tried to get things done without crossing his older brother. Sam believed that in the long run Skip would be a better leader than Tony; he had a "longer fuse" and could quietly lead the employees.

John Griffin understood Sam's dilemma. He felt that the family would best be served by the plan they had developed because it was rational, made business sense, and treated all members of the family fairly. But he was uncomfortable getting in the middle of a family conflict and was concerned about how to get them to discuss the plan while protecting their harmony. Yet as we have seen with previous cases presented earlier in this book, avoiding conflict does not solve problems. In order for the family to implement sound legal and business strategies, their attorney had to play a role in helping them address conflict.

The Importance of Conflict

Most of us are uncomfortable with conflict. We see it as a break-down in relationships and don't like the feeling that someone has to be criticized or feel threatened. Yet conflict is a necessary part of human relationships. Conflict is basically a difference of opinion. It is impossible for two human beings to spend any significant time together without having such differences. The first step to constructive conflict resolution is understanding that conflict is inevitable and even essential for complete, healthy communication. Innovations and improvements rarely occur without conflict. Exhibit 6.1 illustrates this concept with the old story from India about six blind men who try to describe an elephant.

The six blind men had differences of opinion. If each one held to his own view and avoided conflict, he would move through life with a very distorted image of an elephant. When we take the risk of sharing our differences, we give ourselves the opportunity to have more complete and, one hopes, shared perspectives.

Exhibit 6.1. The Elephant's Anatomy.

Six blind men all touched an elephant but each one touched a different part of it. "Oh, the elephant is very flat and thin and has stiff little hairs on one side," said the man touching the elephant's ear. "No," said another, who was touching the elephant's leg. "The elephant is tall and cylindrical and I can almost get my arms around him—like a moving tree trunk." And so on.

If they had collected their observations, their experience, and the assumptions underlying their conclusions, they might have come up with a shared and more complete view of an elephant.

The Advisor's Role in a Conflict Situation

Advisors must understand their own feelings about and experiences with conflict. If they are uncomfortable with conflict themselves then it will be difficult for them to help their clients deal with their situations. If John Griffin could get past his own discomfort with conflict he would offer valuable assistance to his client in implementing a well-designed plan.

Psychologists use the term *countertransference* to describe when a professional projects his or her own feelings or expectations onto a client. In John Griffin's case, he had an older sibling who had always been a bit of a bully. In his family, John learned to argue quite logically about a situation and when doing so failed, to retreat. Thus his older brother often prevailed and John became more and more silently resentful. When John listened to his client's concerns about sibling conflict it unconsciously reminded him of his own childhood relationship. He expected the same kind of negative outcomes and felt uncomfortable about getting involved.

Advisors' first responsibility is to provide the most objective assistance they can and not allow their attitudes to affect the client. So it is appropriate to limit one's involvement in a situation in which one feels unable to maintain one's own boundaries (that is, keep one's personal issues from interfering). At that point, the client would best be served by inviting professional colleagues to collaborate in addressing the situation.

Where and When to Intervene

As we described in Chapter Five, there are multiple interventions available to help a family and business resolve concurrent problems. The sequence of these interventions may vary depending upon the personal and business dynamics at any given point. Similarly, there are many different roles and paths an advisor can take in dealing with conflict.

A useful model is that of public health, which specifies primary, secondary, and tertiary prevention. Primary prevention refers to the prevention of a disease before it occurs; it is what most of us think of as true prevention. Secondary prevention refers to early identification and intervention, that is, preventing the most serious manifestations of the disease by arresting it early. Tertiary prevention refers to treatment of a disorder after it is full-blown with attempts to prevent greater disability or death.

The three stages of the model can be applied to dealing with conflict in family businesses.

Primary prevention. Family business systems experience common developmental challenges that can be anticipated. You can educate your clients about these challenges and help them with the tools to prevent unnecessary conflict, that is, setting up systems to assure fair consideration of all parties and a healthy approach to resolving expected conflict. Such tools include family forums, rules for entry into the business, compensation policies founded on objective financial and business premises, training in constructive conflict resolution, and so on.

Secondary prevention. When communication begins to deteriorate into avoidance or hostility, you can devise interventions to address the immediate issue and identify and resolve the problem in the system (or the individual) that is contributing to the communication breakdown.

Tertiary prevention. When conflict has already caused serious dysfunction in the family or the business, characterized by distrust among members, inability to relate constructively, and possible destruction of the business, you can help your clients look at their options for amicably separating their interests, selling the business, or otherwise halting their destructive paths.

You cannot expect to prevent all conflict. But you can work to prevent destructive, unproductive conflict. As you look for opportunities to prevent, intervene early, or deal with serious manifestations, this model may help you determine where you are most comfortable intervening directly rather than asking for assistance from other professionals. An advisor's ability to handle conflict in a constructive way can resolve many problems and also serve as a model for future problem solving.

Strategies for Constructive Conflict

Advisors can use several strategies to foster constructive resolution of conflict. These are best used in a family retreat or within the format of several ongoing sessions with the family.

Establish a Safe Environment

A safe environment is one in which individuals feel comfortable being authentic and open and taking the risk of bringing up conflicting or controversial perspectives. The leader in a safe environment invites participation and offers a model of openness to the perspectives of others as well as openness with his or her own perspectives. Individuals will become more willing to participate openly as they realize they will be supported rather than criticized, ridiculed, or otherwise censured for such behavior. The advisor's presence, and even the setting of his or her office, can come to represent a safe environment in which the family can explore difficult issues.

One way to set the stage for a safe environment for constructive conflict is to establish and enforce ground rules. Everyone in the family meeting contributes with the understanding that the ground rules will help people feel comfortable being open. Typical ground rules include the following:

- Listen respectfully and don't interrupt.
- Focus on issues, not people or personalities.
- Leave titles outside the door and address one another as peers.
- Offer feedback with consideration and kindness and avoid making attacks.
- Use "I" statements, not "you" statements, as in "I feel irritated and hurt when people interrupt me" rather than "You are so nasty, interrupting me all the time."

Having participants suggest their own ground rules helps to identify and address barriers to openness and to sensitize others to individual concerns.

In safe environments people can also focus on issues instead of on personalities or the manner in which messages are delivered. When people feel attacked, misunderstood, or ignored, they tend to focus on the latter—"You don't know what you are talking about!" or "I don't like the way you said that!" When this kind of reaction occurs, it is often helpful to acknowledge the feelings—"This is a subject that generates a lot of frustration and makes tempers fly"—and refocus attention on the issue at hand—"but let's see if we can get back to the issue and come to a better understanding of each of your positions."

Using a flip chart can help keep everyone focused on the issues. The advisor should write the issue at the top of the page and then create four columns: *Options, Pros, Cons*, and *Remedies for Cons*. At the top of the page the advisor describes the issues or decisions to be made, asking participants to suggest and agree upon them. Next, the advisor lists the range of options presented, encouraging brainstorming, that is, allowing everyone to bring up ideas as they come to mind. Later on all options will be evaluated. Next, the pros and cons of each option are listed and, in the final column, any remedies for the cons are named. Table 6.1 offers an example.

The third way to create a safe environment is to assure that everyone's perspectives are understood and to seek win-win solutions using the techniques described in Chapter Five. Each individual's position can be paraphrased (by the advisor or by others who are asked by the advisor to do so) and described on the flip chart, helping to ensure that all are heard accurately. Many arguments occur because individuals do not feel that others hear or understand them or because people really do misunderstand each other and argue, even when they may hold the same beliefs or positions.

Follow a Systematic Conflict-Resolution Approach

When you determine that you are willing and able to help the family to try to address a conflict, the following steps will help you organize your approach.

Table 6.1. Weighing Options.

Issue: How will we use the profits from last year?

Option	Pros	Cons	Remedies for Cons
Distribute profits to family shareholders.	Family members have money for medical bills, new homes, and so on.	Distribution may restrict company growth.	Use company credit line.
Purchase new equipment for paint line.	Capacity of plant will grow and profits increase next year.	Family will be frustrated with continued sacrifices and limited rewards.	Consider a combination of small dividends and use of a small loan for equipment.

Identify the Issue or Issues.   This is a simple but often overlooked step. People often falsely assume that everyone understands the issue. In fact, sometimes just getting the issue stated clearly eliminates the problem altogether.

Determine Each Party's Motivation to Address the Issue.   What do individuals perceive as the result of not resolving an issue as well as the best possible outcomes? It is also important to assess the level of rigidity or flexibility of each individual and to discuss the need for all parties to commit to making some changes.

Outline the Positions and Options Suggested by All.   Interview each individual privately to identify issues and positions. Having an objective person listen will help defuse some of the intensity and legitimize everyone's right to a position. The interviews can decrease defensiveness and increase openness to dialogue as well as identify points of commonality such as goals, values, assumptions, and so on.

List the Characteristics of an Ideal Outcome.   An ideal outcome would address each party's needs. Find out what the situation would be like if it were resolved to everyone's satisfaction. In other words, what are the criteria for a good decision?

Consider a List of Options.   Consider the pros and cons of all options and whether each will achieve the desired outcome shared by all. The problem-resolution grid of Table 6.1 may be a useful tool in this process.

Select the Best Option.   Help the family select the option that best addresses their description of an ideal outcome. Ask the family to talk about what things would be like if the problem were solved or if the conflict went away. Push family members to propose concrete, detailed visions. This starts the resolution process.

Give an Opportunity to Reflect. It is a good idea to allow time to reflect on the choices made. Ask everyone to "sleep on it" and then be prepared to help the family address concerns they think of later.

Monitor Implementation. The advisor should monitor the implementation of the solution by asking the family to evaluate both how the solution is working and how they feel about the entire conflict-resolution process. If the conflict does not seem to be resolved, then motivation to resolve should once again be addressed. Are forces to maintain the status quo stronger than the motivation to resolve the conflict? Are there patterns in the relationship that need to be addressed in order to break the cycle? It is often useful to diagram the process of the interaction if there is a recurring cycle. Just the awareness of the pattern (again, drawn on a flip chart and kept in view) can help change it. Help the family discuss a representation of the recurring pattern—who repeatedly does what to whom and the usual outcome.

Let's return to the example of John Griffin. John decided he was ready to help Sam work through his concerns so that his estate plan could be implemented. He met with Sam to discuss the fact that he had neither signed the will nor met with the family to discuss his plans. John identified the roadblock: Sam's fear of family conflict. John tried to set Sam at ease by not being judgmental or critical of Sam. He also indicated empathy by explaining that he understood the dilemma, in this case by sharing some parts of his own family dilemma.

John went on to explore possible outcomes if Sam continued to avoid the topic and not complete the planning process. They discussed the risks of Sam's dying intestate and the likelihood of conflict among the heirs and the downfall of the business. Thus Sam's motivation to face the conflict grew. John used a flip chart to list Sam's fears and their underlying assumptions: Tony would be resentful if Sam named Skip successor; Rita would be jealous of her brothers' ownership shares; and all three siblings would end up in conflict.

John and Sam then explored the validity of the assumptions: John did some "wondering aloud" about Sam's conclusions. John volunteered to explore these assumptions in interviews with the children and Helen. He encouraged Sam to keep his ears open for information supporting or refuting his assumptions.

Later on, John met with Tony, Rita, Skip, and Helen to discuss each one's concerns about the business, Sam's plans for it, and their relationships. Through the interview process, John gathered information about their views of the future, their individual roles, potential and actual conflicts, and expectations about ownership of the business. He found that some of Sam's concerns were valid (all felt insecure without a plan and wanted to get things settled while Sam was alive), while others (his concern that there would be jealousy among the children about what each would inherit) did not seem to be. There was a unanimous belief that the business ought to be owned by the active family members, who should buy out Mother and Sister for cash. The estate planning itself was not an issue. However, the leadership of the business was a concern.

After this information-gathering process, John planned a family meeting to discuss estate planning, a subject in which he expected little conflict based upon what he had learned. The meeting was comfortable and helped created the safe environment needed to tackle the more difficult succession issues.

John and Sam then discussed how to involve family business consultants, who could help establish strategic plans, build the family team and address the longer-term needs of the business, the strategic objectives that would meet the financial goals of the owners and career goals of the brothers. At a third family meeting, John outlined remaining challenges, such as succession, and recommended a colleague who could help the family with team building, planning, organizational structure, and relationship issues. He summarized the goals that Sam and his sons had in common: keeping the business in the family with family leadership, further professionalizing the business, allowing for continued careers for both brothers, and maintaining family harmony. He also identified the issues to be resolved and indicated optimism that with professional advice the family could develop strategies to meet their common objectives.

Initiate a Dialogue Process

According to Edgar Schein (1987), social psychologist and professor of management at MIT, "Behind our comments and perceptions there are always assumptions, and our problem-solving process will be improved if we get in touch with our own and each others' assumptions."

Much conflict comes from conclusions based on faulty assumptions. Often a conflict can be resolved simply by making individuals aware of their assumptions. This requires a dialogue. A dialogue process has two phases: an internal phase and an external or sharing phase.

A dialogue starts within each person with an open exploration of the assumptions behind his or her conclusions. This is generally referred to as "listening to the listener," that is, understanding one's own mental models or the steps one went through to reach a conclusion. The second internal step is to question the assumption and realize that it may not be valid.

As long as people don't believe that their assumptions reflect their identities (and do not become overly attached to them and thereby defensive) they can shift perspectives and arrive at shared assumptions. Like the stew that is more than its individual ingredients, shared assumptions become a new view that may make possible a new solution or basis for action.

To begin a dialogue it is useful to note everyone's assumptions on a flip chart and then ponder each in a nonjudgmental manner. The bases for these assumptions should be explored. The advisor may gently inquire whether the assumptions are "safe"—in that they avoid potential conflict—and whether other assumptions might be more valid. Then the advisor works to establish common assumptions by the individuals in conflict. Dialogue can only occur in a safe environment so setting the stage for this kind of communication is important.

Returning to our example, John Griffin used this technique: he encouraged Sam to identify and explore the assumptions underlying his fears. Once these assumptions were on the table, he worked with Sam to explore whether they were valid. As John moved forward with the individual interviews, he identified shared assumptions and used them as a basis for an ongoing dialogue. Then he identified assumptions underlying each individual's position about the future of the business. Where these were in conflict, he noted so, thus preparing the way for continued dialogue about those issues.

Confront "Catastrophizing"

Frequently clients bemoan their situation as being hopeless. They worry that tempers will flair. They feel overwhelmed by the conflicts and difficulties. They avoid dealing with problems that seem impossible to resolve. We call this *catastrophizing*. In fact, without the intrusion of a calm outside objectivity problems may get beyond an ability to be sorted out.

One technique for getting beyond this impasse is to confront the catastrophizing, that is, to challenge the assumption that the situation is impossible. To begin with, the advisor can paraphrase the client's concerns. This may reduce the sense of confusion and feeling of being overwhelmed. It is important not to address the concerns at this point but simply to understand and list them. When the client runs out of steam, the advisor may summarize what has been said and ask, "Is there anything else?" Often, clients are amazed that the advisor not only is not overwhelmed but is seeking more difficulties. This itself reduces the sense of helplessness.

The next step is to sort out the problems and see which ones can be readily resolved: clients usually acknowledge that they can resolve some of the problems, one at a time, on their own. The other problems should be prioritized to help determine which ones the client should tackle first. Finally, the highest priority problems should be reviewed with the systematic problem-solving model suggested in the earlier section of this chapter, while the advisor offers appropriate support or referrals. The client usually actually addresses problems that they previously avoided and then feels much more empowered and comfortable.

Other Strategies

We discuss a range of strategies to prevent and deal with conflict in this book. Many of these techniques help set appropriate expectations in the minds of family business stakeholders. When people have realistic expectations, conflict is less likely to arise.

Typical Family Business Conflicts

A family's conflicts are often rooted in "old baggage"—jealousy, resentment, or feelings of deprivation or obligation. In this section, we describe the most common types of family business conflicts and some techniques for addressing them.

Employment and Exit Policies

Two sisters began resenting an informal policy that women couldn't work in the family business. While the family was working with a financial planner on an estate plan, they raised the issue that it was unfair that their brothers and husbands could work in the company and earn a substantial salary in addition to the distributions all received. The small town they lived in didn't provide many other opportunities for meaningful work. But neither woman possessed skills the company needed. Further, one of the sisters had young children at home and didn't want to work full time, which was required by company policy. Tension was simmering among the siblings and Dad worried about retiring and the tension erupting into major conflict.

Many family business owners and children consider employment in the business a perk of being in the family. This sense of entitlement often extends to the position one expects to have in the business. ("I'm a Hershberg. I have to be one of the top officers. I can't be a lowly clerk; it wouldn't look right.") Some entrepreneurs feel that their children *should* work in the business: it is their legacy and their responsibility to carry it on for the good of the family.

As we will see in Chapter Seven, establishing rules of entry allows families and business managers to make rational and fair decisions that support sound business practices and healthy family functioning. Advisors can urge clients to explore their assumptions about entitlement of family circle members to join the business circle and prod them to think like an owner who is protecting an investment. An advisor may ask, "Who would you rather have in a position—someone who is trained, has excellent experience, and can generate income for the business (and you) immediately? Or someone who feels he or she deserves a job as family member but is not expert in the role and may cost the company rather than generate income for the family?"

A similar technique is empathy training, that is, having owners consider the effect of hiring an unqualified relative on dedicated employees who have worked effectively for several years. The owners may be asked to imagine experienced employees being supervised by a younger person who knows little about the work and, in fact, may hinder productivity. How would the client feel if in the situation of the employee, especially if the young person was earning more than the employee was?

Leaving the business can be as sticky an issue as entering it. This is especially true under several circumstances:

- If a family member is not working well and must be terminated.

- If a family member wants to leave but feels obligated to stay (or believes that he or she doesn't have the skills to work anywhere else, particularly at the salary being earned).

- If an aging founder or senior member of the family is not ready to consider retirement.

Advisors can help clients focus on the separation of roles and realms, that is, on what they do as family members as opposed to what they do as business owners and managers.

Another strategy is to determine whose problem it is. For example, if an individual wants to leave the business but feels obligated to stay is it a personal problem or a business problem? First, it is a personal problem that should be resolved by the individual by calling on any needed professional resources, for example, a psychotherapist or career counselor. When the individual decides to leave, it may become a business issue and the conflict may be addressed in terms of the needs of the business.

Role Definition

Two brothers four years apart in age were faced with their father's imminent and unexpected death. They began to struggle over who should be the successor. The older brother contacted the family accountant, who was helping Dad arrange his estate, to make the case for him to become president; he was the oldest and had worked in the business ten years to his brother's seven. The accountant, who felt loyal to the father, wanted him to be assured that the business would be taken care of and that there would not be strife in the family. He tried to help the sons resolve the issue. He observed that the oldest had an accounting background and knew the financial side of the business, while the younger brother had a marketing background and was more familiar with the customers. The question remained as to who had the leadership capability and the maturity to manage this transition successfully.

The accountant and the father convened an ad hoc advisory group, composed of their banker, a trusted colleague who ran a comparable business in another state, and a major supplier, to discuss the issue. They talked about the leadership needs of the business and gave the father a set of criteria for selection. They went on to recommend the younger son as president and the older as chief financial officer (CFO). Their effective advice helped defuse the situation.

Conflicts can also erupt over who gets to do the "fun" work and who gets perks as well as over how the volume of work is divided. Clarity of roles is a frequent problem: if everyone does everything (as happens in many smaller family businesses), then when something inevitably falls between the cracks, everyone can point a finger at someone else—finding fault, for example, with a family member's job performance.

Process analysis—evaluating what processes the business requires as the basis of job descriptions—can resolve or prevent most of these conflicts. Taking this step helps professionalize a business and can serve as the basis for an organizational philosophy of "continuous improvement," in which competence is the criterion for filling positions and increasing effectiveness is an ongoing expectation. "Protecting the golden goose" is a useful metaphor in resolving many such conflicts. Without competent people in the right roles, the goose may die. Then everyone will suffer.

Who Is in Charge?

The example of the two brothers was first a role issue but second a control issue. Control is a primary source of conflict in family businesses. It can pit owner against manager, old guard against new guard, brother against sister, husband against wife. Who controls decision making, who controls resource utilization, and who arbitrates conflict? The old tradition of primogeniture—in which the eldest son gets all—simplified the control issue. Although it is still the tradition in many family businesses, younger brothers and sisters of all ages are rising to the top or questioning when the eldest automatically is given control.

Control issues are most salient in family businesses where there is lack of trust. The trust issue may be the result of one personality, related to past experience with lack of openness, honesty, or integrity, or related to lack of confidence in one person's competence. Often it is hard for a parent to picture that his or her baby (although the baby is now age forty-five) can manage the business. Family history can also contribute to distrust: "Remember the time I asked you to mow the lawn and it took you two weeks to do it?" "If you lied to me when we were in school, how can I trust that you will be honest with me now?" Differences in values also contribute and this is one reason we emphasize that shared values are an important attribute of successful family businesses. If Dad believes it is important to be loyal to long-term employees even if they are no longer productive but the children are more interested in objective measures of productivity, Dad may not entrust the management of the business to them.

In healthy family businesses, control is shared in an objective, open fashion and conflict over control is less prevalent.

One way to address lack of trust is to discuss the specific underlying causes of the distrust and to explore whether the causes are real or relevant. It is also useful to explore how an individual can earn back lost trust. The advisor may ask, "What would we see if the individual were trustworthy?"

Having control or authority means respect, accountability, and autonomy. Growth of individuals and companies usually requires that control be shared and that authority accompany responsibility. Helping individuals to look at their long-term objectives for the business, the family, and themselves and consider shared control in that context also helps reframe the control issue.

Salary Policies

Some of the most well-known conflicts in family businesses surround the issue of who gets what. Fairness, greed, and entitlement issues are central here. The issues play out in terms of compensation, perks, and use of company assets, ownership, and dividends.

Some family businesses pay all family members the same wages in order to prevent all from feeling that anyone is favored. However, by imposing rules from the family domain (everyone should be treated equally) onto the business domain (salary is based on performance) an equal compensation policy raises expectations that cannot consistently be met and leads to resentments or hostility.

Education about sound business practices provides an objective basis for determining who gets what. For example, the advisor can pose this question to a family member who is not employed in the business but who owns a portion of it: "If the company had a profit of $1 million this year and you, as a one-third owner, could get a distribution of more than $300,000, how would you decide whether to take the cash or reinvest it in the business to buy equipment it needs to grow and potentially yield profits several times higher than what they are now?" This type of question takes family members out of the naive "I deserve" role and puts them into the role of a conscientious owner who must determine how to guide an investment.

When fair market value is the basis for salaries and performance is the basis for bonuses, all employees feel treated fairly and family members are less likely to feel locked into positions for which they are underqualified.

Finally, compensation based on family membership should be in the form of gifts or dividends. Some of this might fly in the face of creative tax management but what it costs in increased taxes is matched by lessened family conflict.

Recognition

A business's core values are most evident in the behaviors that are given recognition through attention paid to the individual, praise, financial reward, promotion, opportunity (for example, offering a position on the board, travel, or additional training), or even a handshake or hug. Even in nonfamily businesses, employees are alert to the values that are manifested in the rewards and recognition given. But family businesses have the additional complication of family dynamics to make the issue more intense: most children seek their parents' approval and recognition, particularly if they have a recognition "deficit" coming out of their childhood. Competition among siblings becomes keen in this arena, often more than in any other. Even adult siblings can be jealous of the attention a sibling receives from Dad or Mom.

In one family, Dad had always dreamed that his four sons would carry on the business he had founded. But Dad needed to control everything and wanted each son to do his bidding. He made his sons compete for his attention and approval, which set up the sons to distrust each other. Even when the sons had reached their forties, they still vied for recognition in more subtle ways, trying to outdo one another with their compulsive spending, fast cars, service on prestigious boards, and wild schemes.

Doing the hard work or being the favorite are other ways children seek recognition or approval from their parents. If recognition supports a clearly articulated statement of family business philosophy, it can minimize destructive conflict and increase organizational effectiveness.

Substance Abuse: A Common Family Business Issue

A recent study of substance abuse in small businesses in Canada found that at least one-third had encountered alcohol and drug abuse among their staffs (*Dealing with Substance Abuse in Small Businesses: Results of a Qualitative Study* [Addiction Research Foundation, 1994]). These problems caused problems in safety, quality of service or product, attendance, management time and energy, productivity, and relations between employees.

In our experience with family businesses, we have found no fewer than one out of two families with alcohol or drug problems. In fact, when a group of ten family business members at a conference recently was asked how many were free of such problems not one person raised a hand.

Few clients come to an advisor's office with a presenting problem of chemical dependency. But many transactions involving advisors will no doubt be affected by substance abuse in the client's family. The following fictional anecdote is an example.

Jeff Gordon, CFO of the Blank Box Company, calls Martha Stromberg and asks to meet for lunch. Martha is the senior partner of a regional accounting firm and has worked with the Blank Box Company for twenty-three years. Since Jeff joined the company, two years ago, Martha has had less day-to-day contact with the owners (two brothers) and has been focusing on estate planning, retirement planning, and helping to establish sources of financing for expansion.

Over lunch Jeff confides in Martha that he is quite concerned about Stan, the older brother, who has been drinking more and more heavily. He has been putting away quite a bit on the weekends for some time, but now he is also drinking during lunch, sometimes coming back to work in a rage. Sarge, the younger brother, is fearful of confronting Stan. Stan is already threatened by Sarge's attempts to expand the company in new directions. Sarge is concerned that if he brings up the drinking issue, Stan may feel he is just trying to push him out. Jeff knows that employees are beginning to be affected by Stan's behavior. Jeff appeals to Martha to intervene because she has worked closely with both brothers for several decades. Furthermore, the work she is doing with them now could be disrupted by Stan's problem.

Martha is not happy to hear this news. She has seen Stan in an inebriated state at their club on weekends. She knows that she will have to find a way to deal with the problem.

Many other situations involving advisors are affected by substance abuse in the client's family. Here are some examples:

- An owner would like to leave the business in his son's hands but suspects he's still using marijuana and thus can't be depended on.

- The president of a company is putting his business at risk. He has drink after drink at lunch and his clients are losing faith in him and the business. The president sees his drinking as part of entertaining clients.

- An owner is afraid to leave any of his estate to his daughter, who drinks a lot, eats compulsively, and, he claims, goes out with "questionable" men. He wonders whether he can leave money in trust to his grandchildren without insulting his daughter.

- A family gathered to discuss planning will not freely discuss any issues. They seem to have serious concerns but there is a conspiracy of silence. In fact, they are reluctant to mention their fears about Mom's drinking. They are afraid that if they speak openly about it the whole family and the business will unravel.

This is just a sample of some explosive issues that can arise during the process of interacting with a family business. After advisors deal with the first set of business or estate issues, they usually begin to see the substance abuse issues. As families become more comfortable with them, they become more open.

Once again, we assert that our intent in this book is not to turn our readers into therapists or chemical dependency counselors. Instead, we seek to help you recognize the signs of substance abuse and suggest ways to help families get help.

Understanding the Nature of Substance Abuse

What distinguishes substance abuse from use? The addicted person uses a substance (including alcohol, drugs, food) compulsively and rigidly denies that he or she has a problem. Compulsiveness is defined as the irrational, illogical, irresponsible, and continued use of a substance (or habit, including work), despite adverse consequences. This type of use is often evidenced by the way in which the substance is used:

- Lying about how much, when, and where the substance is used (minimizing the use)
- Guarding a supply to ensure it will always be available
- Thinking about and using a substance inappropriately (making it the center of one's life)
- Taking alcohol or drugs as self-prescribed medication (to sleep or calm nerves, for example)
- Driving, appearing in public, or telephoning while in an altered state of consciousness
- Trying to "cure" oneself by changing brands or the places where the substance is used
- Continuing use despite warning from people the individual loves and respects

Chemical dependency is a progressive disorder that becomes more and more debilitating. What makes it so hard to treat is denial: "I don't have a problem," "I can stop any time," "Leave me alone, it is none of your business," "I still go to work and have a job, don't I?" The denial of people around chemically dependent people helps to perpetuate the problem; this is called *enabling*. Family members or colleagues may cover up for an alcoholic by saying that the individual is sick and won't be at work today or by making other excuses for the person's behavior ("She's under a lot of pressure with those kids of hers and her job"). They often compensate for the drug-dependent person by looking after the individual's responsibilities, hoping "this too shall pass." That a family member might be an alcoholic is unthinkable to many.

Because of the pervasive impact on the entire family, chemical dependency is considered to be a family disease. In family businesses with a chemical dependency, most of the family is affected in one way or another.

Patterns of Deterioration in the Workplace

Chemically dependent people bring their problems to work. As the disease progresses, it becomes harder and harder to cover it up. Maintaining a job is an important aspect of denial. If people can point to the fact that they are still meeting the responsibilities of work—evidenced by their not being fired—the denial can continue. That is why confrontation by employers is one of the most effective strategies for interrupting the cycle of chemical dependency.

Chemically dependent employees progressively deteriorate in their capacity to handle their job. The following behaviors, when they occur over time, demonstrate this kind of deterioration:

- Absenteeism and tardiness increase along with improbable excuses.
- Problems with concentration and confusion yield lower productivity, higher error rates, poor judgment, and lowered efficiency.
- Work performance becomes irregular, characterized by periods of high and low effort and time spent intensely at work or absent altogether.
- Personality suggests a mood-affected condition (for example, giddiness, blurred speech, irritability, or paranoid behavior).
- Relations with customers and co-workers deteriorate because of overreaction to real or imagined criticism, mood and attitude swings, and an increasing lack of money and need to borrow money.

Any of these behaviors alone is not an indication of chemical dependency. A pattern of such behaviors and increased evidence of them over time is.

When these issues occur in a family business, it is even more complicated than when they occur in another type of workplace. Dad may want to deny the problem and believe his son when he says he's "cured" even when evidence to the contrary is present. Employees are less likely to bring up problematical behavior because it involves "the boss's kid." When brother or sister brings up the problem, it is attributed to sibling rivalry. Thus denial and avoidance of the problem can be especially troublesome in a family business.

Intervention Processes

Chemically dependent people must overcome one of the most difficult aspects of the disease in order to get help: denial. This may happen when they hit bottom—when the spouse leaves, the kids get into trouble, they are terminated from work, or health fails—or when the most important people in their life confront them with overwhelming evidence of the disease. The latter is an intervention.

Interventions should be conducted by a professional with training in the process. In essence, the spouse, children, employer, extended family, clergy, friends, or associates gather and tell the individual what each has observed as alcoholic or drug-related behavior, how it has hurt them individually, that they still care about the individual, and that they want the individual to get help.

When a person is surrounded by all the significant people in his or her life describing specific incidents and their impact on them, it is very difficult to continue to deny the problem. Arrangements are usually made before the intervention with a treatment professional or facility for immediate help, before denial creeps back in.

The families also need to understand the disease of addiction, have an opportunity to deal with its impact on their lives, and learn what they have done to encourage the chemical dependency and how to help the chemically dependent person stay in recovery.

Advisors may help the family do these things in several ways. They may help them identify that there is a problem that, unaddressed, will become more serious for the individual, the family, and the business and indicate that help is available. They may confront the individual with their observations as part of the intervention team. They may help the family identify treatment resources. They may discuss business law issues regarding substance abuse, such as company policies and practices for compliance with the Drug Free Workplace Act (which mandates that employees sign an affidavit that they are not using drugs), drug and alcohol testing and treatment policies, and liability for employee job performance "under the influence."

Let's return to Martha and her work with the Blank Box Company. Martha decides to explore the situation a bit more on her own. She invites the Blank brothers to lunch at the club to discuss their planning in order to have an opportunity to observe Stan firsthand. As she had feared, he drinks heavily and becomes more and more irritable and demanding during the lunch. Sarge grows more uncomfortable and gives Martha pained looks from time to time.

After the lunch, Martha meets with Sarge to discuss her observations. Sarge notes that Stan's wife, also in her sixties, has been avoiding the situation by going away to visit their children who live in other parts of the country. When she is away, Stan drinks even more heavily. Martha asks if Stan has had a physical exam in recent years and if their physician is aware of the problem. Sarge doesn't know but thinks such an exam would be a good step. A physical will be required for the insurance program they are developing so Martha can encourage Stan to get that done first.

Martha and Sarge agree that after the physical they will talk with Stan about their concerns, particularly if the feedback from the doctor indicates physical deterioration resulting from alcohol abuse. Martha says she is willing to talk about her observations at lunch and at the club on weekends. She suggests that Sarge speak with a local chemical dependency specialist about coping with Stan and how they might confront him in a constructive manner. She suggests that it would be helpful for Sarge to have that support no matter what Stan's ultimate decision turns out to be.

Treatment Resources

Each community has a range of professionals who can assist with treatment of chemical dependency. They include addictionologists (physicians who specialize in addiction), chemical dependency counselors (nonmedical counselors who specialize in addictive disorders), clinical social workers, marriage and family counselors, and psychologists and psychiatrists. Private and public hospitals frequently offer inpatient and sometimes outpatient treatment programs as well. These vary in quality. However, at a minimum they should be approved by the Joint Commission on the Accreditation of Hospitals (JCAH), have dedicated chemical dependency staffs, offer medical supervision, and have programs that involve the whole family and provide thorough aftercare assistance.

Another source are Alcoholics Anonymous (AA) and Narcotics Anonymous (NA). These self-help organizations provide meetings for chemically dependent individuals along with extensive educational programming. AA and NA are excellent adjuncts to other forms of treatment. For individuals who are highly motivated to address their chemical dependency, AA or NA may be enough. Programs based on the one developed by AA have been created for people with eating disorders (Overeaters Anonymous), compulsive gambling (Gamblers Anonymous), and other compulsive disorders.

Sister organizations Al-Anon and Narc-Anon establish self-help groups for family members or significant others concerned with their loved ones' chemical dependency or their own reactions to it. There are even programs for teen offspring (Al-a-Teen) and younger children (Al-a-Tot). If clients are concerned about their chemically dependent loved ones and can't get them to seek help, they may still find attendance at Al-Anon or Narc-Anon beneficial.

The local AA or NA chapter (listed in the telephone directory) may also be a good source of information on clinical resources for treatment in a community. In addition, the National Association of Independent Interventionists may be able to help in the search for a specialist to conduct an intervention. This organization provides regional listings of individuals who are trained and certified to conduct interventions.

Given the number of family businesses that are troubled by substance abuse in one form or another, you will probably not escape an encounter with this problem. If you ignore the problem, you too will enable the individual or the family to continue a downhill slide. Clients may not always like the advice they are given, but an ethical stand is to deliver observations and recommendations and allow the clients to decide how to respond. Even if your clients ignore your observations in the short run, they may eventually help make it more difficult to perpetuate denial. Because families with members who are overinvolved with alcohol or drugs find it difficult to proceed with other significant plans, addressing substance abuse may be important to the success of your work.

Summary

In this chapter we discussed the nature of conflict, the advisor's role in intervening in conflict, and some techniques for dealing with conflict. Conflict is a natural part of life and is important. It allows us to work with others and to be creative. If we can befriend conflict we can better assist family businesses work through the challenges of their development.

Here are some general thoughts on dealing with conflict:

- Remain objective; it is easy to become one person's advocate before hearing "the rest of the story."

- Don't assume the situation is as grave as it appears. It may feel more dire to participants than it really is, given the right outside assistance.

- Listen to your "gut." If the situation feels beyond your capability, gracefully get out and find other assistance.

- Be a role model in identifying and facing conflict: your comfort will help your clients.

The next chapter looks at the design of structures to manage the complex web of family and business relationships.

Chapter Seven

Creating Boundaries, Structures, and Policies

Families divide up responsibility for, authority over, and ownership of their business. Over time, they redefine and reorganize these relationships. When families fight, it is often over expectations, values, and rights concerning the business. When family members have appropriate forums to voice their concerns, conflict may be avoided, managed, or minimized.

In this chapter we explore how family business advisors can help their clients establish clear boundaries between family and business, create structures to manage different stakeholders' divergent interests, and establish and clarify relationships. This chapter will help experts better understand the family system and how it affects a family's ability to make decisions and take action. It will offer some tools with which to begin to expand the family's definition of what's important and what they need to do. This chapter will help advisors help families deal with their business issues and develop effective boundaries and governing structures.

Balancing Stakeholder Needs

Family members have a stake in their family's business whether or not they own shares or work there. People who do not work in the business but own stock may have as much at stake and be as personally and emotionally invested in the business as those who do. However, they often view financial issues quite differently (favoring short-term returns) from family managers or owners (often favoring reinvestment of profits for future growth or being concerned with the status in the community that comes from the family business). Similarly, individuals who are directly related to owners or managers of the business tend to have different perspectives about the business than individuals who have married into the family.

The following list represents the categories of stakeholders who may have divergent desires and needs in a family business system:

- Family members who work in the business and own stock
- Family members who own stock but don't work in the business
- Family members who work in the business but don't own stock
- Family members who don't work in the business and don't own stock
- Key nonfamily managers who may or may not own stock
- Spouses and children of family members in the above groups

The overlapping relationships between owners, family members, managers, and employees are depicted in Figure 7.1.

Whether you enter a client relationship as an expert advisor informed by family dynamics or as a process consultant, you may find yourself caught between competing interests of different groups. Your challenge is to seek ways to benefit the interests of all the stakeholders.

A family systems-informed expert can help the family create a system of structures and policies that balances the different needs of stakeholders and understand the broader set of considerations that go into an effective business decision. A process consultant might take a more direct role in creating and implementing such structures and policies.

Whichever consulting style you assume, all your efforts should lead to reaching the critical goal of helping groups of stakeholders raise and resolve their different interests, concerns, problems, and conflicts.

Figure 7.1. Overlapping Stakeholder Interests.

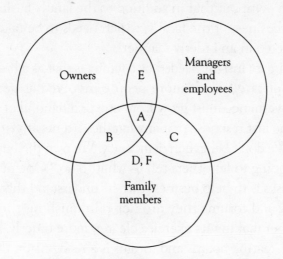

Source: Adapted from John Davis and Renate Tasiuri.

Creating Business Structures

Many family businesses only meet in a sort of ad hoc group of family members who own and work in the business. These groups usually don't meet regularly, do not keep minutes of meetings, and have such divergent ideas of individual roles and responsibilities that they often fail to make them explicit among themselves.

Whatever professional role you take, you will find that working in the family-business interface demands that family members clarify their roles and the nature of their involvement. We have seen lawyers, accountants, and management consultants help families organize family boards and financial planners help them organize family forums. As you become more aware of the family dynamics and the nature of the family business, you too may want to help the family organize itself.

The family may be thought of as a large organization with precise and demanding psychological and economic responsibilities. One is to oversee and manage the business interests and assets, which may include real estate and a portfolio of investments. The advisor can point out that in addition to the family business, there is also the business of the family, which needs to be taken care of and conducted in an orderly manner.

The primary insight needed by a family is that as a business gets more complicated, with more people involved as generations mature, governance must grow from one or a handful of people to several. The first response of many families is a negative one. They may say, "We don't believe in democracy. We own the business and we're not going to let others tell us what to do." One of the advisor's key tasks is to help business owners understand that by creating boards and forums they are not relinquishing their formal authority but making its exercise clearer, more orderly, and more effective. Creating boards and forums is a recognition that power will eventually shift and that it can be more effective if the people who eventually hold it are well prepared. First and foremost, these governing structures enhance communication. Only secondarily are they decision-making structures. Although sometimes difficult, it is important to persuade business owners that the time has come to discuss family and business affairs more openly.

The specific structures can vary. We present two models that may be offered for consideration to families. The exact form adopted will be up to the family and must fit its particular situation. The first model is for businesses with annual revenues of up to roughly $100 million that contain one or no more than two generations of a single family. When a business gets larger than this, contains more branches of a family, or employs more than about a dozen family members with different roles and responsibilities, the family may need to adopt the more complex structure of the second model.

Three Core Structures

Whichever model chosen, three core structures are needed. The first is the *family forum*, which attends to the business of the family.

It is the basic body that governs and regulates the family. It usually includes all family members over a certain age, such as fourteen, and includes spouses. This group should meet at least once a year for a lengthy meeting. An executive committee produces a newsletter as well as written minutes of the annual meeting and its decisions. Operating rules for this body should be defined in what we call a *family charter*. (See the last section of this chapter for more on this.)

The second core structure is a board. This group may take the form of *family board* (for smaller companies) or *board of directors* (for larger firms). The board deals with the business of the business. As a business gets larger and more complex, there may be nonfamily owners and legal and business considerations that lead to the formation of the more formal board of directors. A family board has more to do than a board of directors because in smaller family businesses matters such as how family members get hired, evaluated, compensated, and treated go beyond the usual considerations of the board of directors.

The third core structure is an *advisory board*. We recommend that in addition to family members, at least three professionals from different disciplines who are neither members of the family nor employees of the family business sit on this board. One nonfamily member should have a strong background in finance. Other positions may be allocated to marketing, manufacturing, real estate—any areas of expertise that are lacking in family board members and the management team.

The Executive Function

In addition to these three core structures, all businesses, large and small, new and old, have an executive function consisting of the chief executive officer (CEO) or president. This individual often works together with a management team to operate the business and reports to the family board or board of directors. The top management team often includes both family and nonfamily members. It is important to differentiate this group, which deals with operations and management, from the board, which sets policy and direction. In practice, especially in smaller businesses, the two groups may overlap, but it is important to recognize that their functions are different and separate.

Figures 7.2 and 7.3 compare the proposed mediating structures of small and large family businesses. Although the two are similar, the larger family business contains additional entities to manage its more complex functions.

Stage One Companies

Small businesses—those employing one or two generations with few stakeholders and revenues under $100 million—benefit from the establishment of these three core structures.

Family Forum. All family members older than age fourteen, including those who marry into the family, belong in this group whether they own shares or work in the business. The family forum should create a comfortable learning environment in which all feel

Figure 7.2. Stage One Family Business Structures.

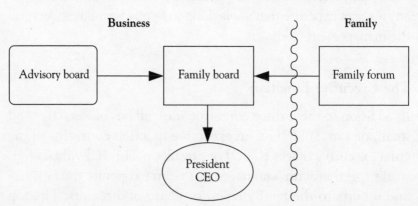

free to express themselves, as described in the two preceding chapters. One family member (preferably someone other than the chair
of the family board or the key corporate executive) should be
responsible for administering the forum for each term, with the
leadership changing periodically. The leader establishes the agenda,
makes arrangements for meetings, and coordinates such outside
resources as speakers and facilitators.

The family forum becomes the primary mechanism for exploring all family issues, especially those relating to the boundaries
between family and business.

In order to build a consensus of understanding and familywide
support for those active in the business, a family forum is best used
for debate, discussion, and education, leaving decision making up
to those who are actively engaged in the business and serve on the
family board. However, there is some overlap of members on the
forum and the board.

The family forum gives a legitimate venue to the family efforts
to nurture family members, helping them develop self-esteem,

Figure 7.3. Stage Two Family Business Structures.

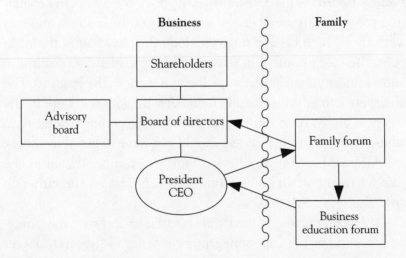

independence, and life skills such as communication skills, interpersonal skills, and business and management skills.

The family forum's annual meeting should review general business concepts, the company's financial statements, estate planning, charitable giving, and other pertinent matters. The meeting should follow a prepared agenda, set time limits, and perhaps include outside resources or educators. Topics should be limited to the big picture, trends, and significant changes. Under no circumstances should forum members debate operating matters—the day-to-day details of management, hiring, and detailed business activities. To do so would violate the boundary between owner prerogatives and prerogatives that must be delegated to the management team. Oversight should not be allowed to evolve into meddling in the business.

Early forum meetings should be devoted to the creation of a statement of purpose. One family forum stated its purpose in this way: "To raise the level of general business knowledge, understanding, and acumen of all family members so that they will be prepared to act responsibly should they be faced with important decisions."

Family Board. This decision-making body consists of the ownership group, family members who own part of the business and may work there. Membership might include the president of the company, the vice president of sales, the vice president of operations, and a minority shareholder who does not work in the business. The chairperson might be a family member who does not work in the business but owns stock, the retired founder perhaps. Long-term advisors to the family business should not serve as board members.

All board members, whether family or nonfamily, should be paid for their participation. Compensation is usually on either an annual or a per-meeting basis.

The main purpose of the family board is to deal with the family-business and ownership-management interface issues and to steer the business. The board should provide an appropriate way for stakeholders to participate in the business. It should help guide the family's way of relating and making business decisions toward the practical rather than the emotional. Lines of communication between the board and the family forum should be open, allowing for free exchanges between the two groups. Other purposes of the board are to balance power among the various systems by investing power in the board as an institution rather than in individual members, to depersonalize the formula for business success, to base decisions on consensus, to promote team building, to represent a stable structure in times of crisis, to provide the structure for transition of the business to future generations, and to create a foundation for the group to move forward.

The board can manage the entry of family members into the business. Through the family forum, each family should create a set of criteria for employment by family members. The board should provide a clear boundary between family business owners who may or may not work in the business but have voting rights and responsibilities and other family members who may work in the business but do not own shares.

The board will achieve long-term success by balancing three competing needs: the capital needs of the business, the liquidity needs to meet the family's own financial demands, and the needs of the owners to maintain control of the business.

At first the board should meet on a frequent basis (monthly or quarterly) to gain momentum and to get organized. Meetings should focus on developing the various documents and assigning individual members specific responsibilities and time frames in which to accomplish them. At subsequent meetings, members should present their results for review by the board as a whole. Initial goals for the group are to experience success working together around positive goals and to begin to define internal relationships based on performance of specific tasks as members of a team. After a while this process should become a formal planning process.

A formal planning process is used in most professionally managed companies and is based on the business mission statement. The plan includes financial, performance, and special-project goals. The board should divide the plan and allocate components to business units responsible for their implementation. This process should be delegated all the way down to the lowest levels of the organization. Each business unit should have its own plan that is integrated into the overall plan. The board should review progress on these plans at its regular meetings. Once a year the entire process is renewed by reviewing the business mission statement, fine-tuning the long-range plan, and establishing new plans for the upcoming year.

The development of the plan is a collaborative process, but once in place all participants are responsible for achieving their pieces of it. As long as progress is satisfactory the board does little more than consult and advise. If substantial deviations occur, the board becomes more involved to remedy the situation. This process has additional benefits:

- It communicates the direction of the company to all the stakeholders.
- It provides the basis for a compensation system based upon business success rather than more subjective criteria.
- It clarifies the relationship of family employees—especially the company president—with their employers—the board.
- It increases the accountability of family member employees.
- It gets the family to define the strategic niche of the business.
- It helps the family focus on making the business successful and gives a specific road map for achieving success.

The board should also develop a planning calendar to include an annual family work session (for more on this see Chapter Five) and a planning sequence tied to the fiscal year. One possible scenario is for the board to meet quarterly and have two additional meetings with the family forum. The last meeting may be tied to a year-end review and projections for the coming year.

Advisory Board. In addition to the first two core groups, an advisory board is also needed. This group of business professionals meets regularly and advises the business. Its carefully selected members should include professionals from the community who are close to the owners and trusted by the owners but who have the courage and strength of character (and no conflicts of interest) to tell the truth and to pose hard questions. They can help with difficult family dilemmas, such as choosing a successor for the business, mentoring or evaluating the qualifications of family members to serve in the business. Giving this group an advisory status helps minimize the legal liability of members of the board of directors. However, business leaders should carefully prepare for advisory board meetings by sharing information and formulating major issues and choices.

Stage Two Companies

Older and larger family businesses, which include two, three, or more generations and several nuclear families and generate annual sales greater than $100 million are best served by formal mediating structures.

Family Forum. Like the forum for Stage One companies, the Stage Two family forum should include all family members, including spouses and older children. When families limit membership to lineal descendants and exclude spouses, they create a divisive mentality. Setting an age, such as fourteen, as a level of entry to the forum also can serve as a rite of passage, a time when family members begin to learn how to handle confidential matters.

As a business grows to involve more and more generations and branches of the family, the forum may create additional structures for specific functions. A steering committee acts as executive team and plans an annual meeting. A second subgroup of the forum can act as an entry point into the business and help train future family leaders. This subgroup can speed up and facilitate the transition process into the business and mediate family business disputes. The family forum may also create an educational forum to teach family members about the business and about communication and problem-solving methods. An accountant who is advising the family might urge the creation of an educational forum to teach financial analysis and investment theory or such practical skills as how to read a spread sheet. An attorney might offer a session on corporate law, the prerogatives of shareholders, and fiduciary responsibility of trustees; such a session may become a recurring activity.

At the root of the dismantling of some large and well-known family businesses are often differing assumptions and premises of the individual family members. Although a family forum cannot guarantee harmony, it provides an opportunity for members to learn to work together, discuss different views, discover common goals, create common assumptions, and perhaps resolve their differences and focus on the positive aspects of owning an enterprise.

Board of Directors. This formally structured governing body contains elected representatives of family owners as well as outside members. Like a family board, the board of directors is charged with solving problems and making decisions to enhance the interests of those whose money is on the line—the owners of the company, including minority shareholders. The board has ultimate responsibility for the success of the business. It is responsible for establishing long-range direction, setting goals, and monitoring progress.

The responsibilities of the board include the same ones as those of the family board in Stage One companies. Both groups have legal and fiduciary responsibility for setting and meeting strategic goals. The main difference between the two is that here the family has grown too large for all to serve on the board. The business requires professional managers, and the board required outside expertise as well. As a family business grows in size and sophistication, the family board can evolve into this more formal structure.

There is another difference. In Stage One companies all family members through the family forum usually elect representatives to sit on the family board. In Stage Two companies only shareholders (whether or not a part of the family) elect the board of directors.

The most common impediments to the success of a board are members who are not team players. Such behavior must be confronted—a task that often falls to the advisor. Uncooperative members may behave better in a more public setting with nonfamily advisors present. It is also important for advisors to remember that they too often press for absolute harmony when a more appropriate goal would be working effectively together. Most other challenges, including death and divorce, can be worked through. Indeed, the value of the board is most clearly demonstrated during such crises.

A family forum can define policies for the family and suggest business policies to the board of directors. The board can choose to adopt the policies or modify them. The family forum can also recommend candidates outside the business and the family to sit on the board of directors. As already noted, only shareholders can legally elect members of the board. But family forum members can suggest candidates, helping create a consensus process in the selection.

A key difficulty in family business advising is that lines of communication and authority tend to flow from family managers to the board or from the family to the business without respect for each family member's appropriate role. By separating family and business issues, an advisor can help establish healthy boundaries and make sure that decision-making power rests solely with the board. Many families resist involving outsiders in the business and the prevailing norm in some families is not to share financial information with anyone, even other family members, who are outside the business. It therefore is not always possible to organize all stakeholders into mediating structures although that should be the ideal to which every advisor aspires.

In one example, a large family that has operated a holding company with many businesses for more than five generations has formed a family forum that meets annually. The family's large and complex organization has a charter and rules of operation. It contains several hundred family members who own part of the holding company. Only a handful of family members work in the business. The family forum elects a leader for a set term of office and an executive steering committee. When family members reach age fourteen and when people marry into the family they are invited to the annual orientation session, at which time they are introduced to the family holding company. Family forum meetings include educational seminars, strategic planning sessions, and discussions of family and business issues. The result is clarity in this family's ability to separate family issues from business issues and to manage the business and work as a family.

The focus is on helping the family use rational rather than emotional ways of relating. The planning process is used as the foundation to assure the success of the business and to provide an objective basis for communication, problem solving, and decision making.

Creating Organizational Policies

Once the business structures are in place, advisors can focus on helping their clients clarify organizational policies.

Rules of Entry

One of the family forum's most important tasks is to develop and recommend policies to the board that concern the interface between the family and the business. Sooner or later, almost every owner has to decide whether to hire a family member. This problem becomes critical in the second and third generations of a business, when there are more and more family members to consider. The following anecdote illustrates how the lack of an entry policy can erode family ties and business performance. A management consultant might have tried to carve out more explicit roles and create better management coordination and supervision but such changes would have conflicted with the family's philosophy.

Brothers David and Leon started a manufacturing business forty years ago. Their sons all grew up in the business, visiting often and working there as soon as they were old enough. A family rule stated that the business was for everyone and everyone was expected to work there. When David's three sons and Leon's two sons finished college and entered the company, the business was starting to change. Competitors were emerging and new marketing tools were needed. Leon, who handled marketing, increasingly took the leadership role, although nominally the two founding brothers were equal. As the sons entered the business, the ad hoc nature of its organization frustrated them. Cousins and brothers tripped each other up. A young cousin was expected to teach the business to an elder who had just arrived from business school.

Authority structures were generational and lines of authority between siblings and cousins just didn't work. Tensions grew between David's traditionalism and Leon's vision. Furthermore, Leon's oldest son, Ray, was not aggressive or far-seeing, while David's second son, Andy, had all the necessary skills to be a successor to Leon. The two families began to feud. This kind of dilemma can manifest itself in many different ways. One son of a family founder reports: "Dad always wanted me to join the business and spoke as if there were no other choices for me. I sometimes wonder if this is the best thing for me . . . but I've been here since high school and I don't know if I could get hired anywhere else."

A young woman in her thirties admits, "My grandfather founded our business and never considered the possibility that his 'girls' would join the business. But when my father and uncles began looking at our generation of six to eight children who could be employed by the business, they decided we should all have the chance. I wasn't at all interested in joining the business. However, after I finished graduate school, it seemed almost disloyal not to use my skills within the family. Now I feel that I got the job because of my ability not my family ties."

"Well, I'm really frustrated!" says a third person we have worked with. "I worked my way up to a management position in our business after six years here. Now, they've brought in my cousin, who has no experience and he's getting the same salary I'm getting. But he's not contributing his share to the bottom line!"

A Family Charter.　These family employees are trying to cope with overlapping roles, expectations, and values of two systems—family and business—and the conflicts that can result. The most constructive route to balancing these responsibilities, opportunities, and needs is to develop guidelines for entry into the family business. Guidelines provide an objective basis for deciding which family members can join the business. The rules for entry can complement the family and business mission statements and form a central part of the family charter.

The most important rule for employment by a family business is that it be based on a clear, consistently applied policy. The guidelines depend in part on the nature of the family and business, their missions, their size, the industry, and the resources available. Guidelines should address the following five issues.

Who is eligible to join? Some family businesses limit employment to nonfamily members, believing that this strategy eliminates most conflicts, but maintain ownership of the business as an asset of family members. Other eligibility issues include those relating to employment of spouses, in-laws, or cousins by marriage. In all cases, family members should not be hired because of family ties but because they have the ability to contribute to the business.

What are the criteria for entry? Exposing youngsters to the business through summer jobs during high school can be beneficial but permanent, full-time employment straight out of high school or college is unwise. Guidelines should specify the age, education, and experience needed by family members before they can apply.

A twenty-one-year-old generally lacks sufficient maturity to handle the web of family dynamics and business stressors in a family business. Nevertheless, a business may want to impose an age limit by which time a family member must join. This encourages long-term commitment and avoids letting the business be seen as a security blanket to use when all else fails.

We recommend requiring a minimum of three to five years of outside experience prior to joining the family business. At least one of those jobs should last two years or more and include a promotion. Outside experience helps family members develop business competence and confidence and enhances the contribution they can make to the business.

Is there a job opening? The business should only offer family members positions that fill a clear business need and for which the candidate is qualified. It is unwise to create unnecessary positions simply to employ a family member. Doing so leads to resentment among other employees and does little for the self-esteem of the person involved. The only exception occurs when a successor is being groomed and is transferred from one position or project to another in order to learn different aspects of the business.

Is there supervision? Once family members are hired, they should be supervised by a nonfamily manager to decrease subjectivity of evaluation and feedback. Whenever possible, the family employee, especially if on a leadership track, should also have a designated mentor outside the immediate family who can provide guidance and feedback.

Are there conditions of continued employment? Some family businesses don't hold family employees accountable for their performance and pay them more than they could earn in the outside world. Others expect family employees to work harder and receive less compensation than other employees. Family members should be held to minimum standards of performance and receive fair market compensation.

For example, the four Wilson brothers owned a business with gross sales of nearly $50 million annually. Founded by their parents, the business provided well for all the brothers. But the brothers had deep concerns about succession and employing the third generation—of which there were twenty-seven members. One member of the younger generation was already employed by the company and others were knocking on the door. The Wilson brothers asked an advisor to help them develop a family employment policy that would meet their circumstances. They needed tough, clear rules that would protect the company, which they laughingly called "the Golden Goose."

The policy created was formally set down in what we call a family charter. It reflected their long-term goal (prudent stewardship of the family enterprise) and the family's values (education, competence, self-esteem, independence, church, and community).

The family charter developed by the Golden Goose Company, as we will call it, may help other family businesses come up with their own. In the following paragraphs we provide the actual policy of this large and complex family business. We often use it as a vehicle for discussion to help family businesses begin to formulate their own policy. Advisors can give a copy of the Golden Goose's policy to a client family and ask them to see if it helps them identify the areas their own family needs to regulate. Families can also try to write down what policies and practices exist right now. Then they can assess and reflect on them.

The Golden Goose Family Charter

Purpose. The purpose of this policy is to define the procedures, process, and criteria that will govern how Wilson family lineal descendants and their spouses enter and exit from the family company's employ. This employment policy is intended to remove the ambiguity that currently exists so that interested family members can shape their career paths accordingly. We believe that clear, constructive communication of this policy will contribute to the long-term success of our family and the Golden Goose Company.

Philosophy. We are a family committed to our members and descendants being responsible, productive, and well-educated citizens who practice the work ethic and make constructive contributions to the local community and the world at large. Each member is encouraged to develop and use marketable skills that contribute to the enhancement of his or her self-esteem and independence. We believe that for a family member to be employed in this company there must be a legitimate job available and the skills to match.

It is the policy of this company to search out and employ at all levels individuals who have the ability to manage vertical and horizontal relationships, who show evidence of ability and willingness to take initiative, who exhibit self-confidence and high self-esteem, and who are both independent and responsible in managing their lives and their jobs.

We subscribe to the philosophy that the opportunity to be employed in our company be earned; it is not a birthright. Our business succeeds when professional competence is the criterion for entrance to employment. Further, high-level competence must be supported by a sustained performance record. We believe that family members who cannot meet these standards will be happiest employed elsewhere.

General Conditions. The following paragraphs state the general conditions for employment and employment performance.

1. Family members must meet the same criteria for hiring as nonfamily applicants.
2. Family members are expected to meet the same level of performance required of nonfamily employees. Like nonfamily employees, they will be subject to performance reviews and to the same rules regarding firing.
3. As a general principle, family members will be supervised by nonfamily members.

4. Family members under age thirty are eligible for temporary employment with "temporary" defined as less than one year. To be reemployed after this term family members must meet the requirements of Condition 7 following.

5. No family member may be employed in a permanent entry-level position (that is, a position that requires no previous experience or training).

6. Compensation will be at fair market value for all positions held.

7. Family members seeking permanent employment must have at least five years of work experience outside this company. One of those jobs must have been of at least three years' duration with the same employer, during which time there must have been at least two promotions. It is our view that if a family member is not a valued employee elsewhere then it is not likely he or she will be happy or useful in the Golden Goose Company.

Application for a Position. Family members must make their interest known in writing to the president and chief executive officer of the Golden Goose Company. When a position becomes available, only family members who have expressed an interest in writing will be informed of it. They may then complete the normal application forms and submit the application for appropriate processing and consideration.

Succession. The size of our company necessitates our reliance on nonfamily professionals. These industry leaders bring fresh ideas to our business and, thus, renewal to our family and to our business. To provide incentive for these employees to excel and to aspire to the presidency of our company, we will alternate the position of president between a family member and a nonfamily employee. No family member can succeed another family member as president and chief executive officer of the Golden Goose Company.

Education. Each quarter there will be a family meeting to report on the status of the Golden Goose Company. This meeting will be open to all spouses and to extended-family members age fourteen and older. It will follow an educational model, with segments of the meeting geared to different levels of understanding. The purpose will be to develop throughout the extended family a broad-based high-level understanding of business. Financial matters and asset management will be heavily emphasized. Learning how to handle confidential family matters will be part of the education process. One of these meetings will be called the Golden Goose Annual Family Gathering. It will include outside presenters, offer interesting learning opportunities, and include other activities to enhance and enrich our family life.

If a family member has not already earned a master's degree at the time of permanent employment, he or she must earn one in a business-related field within six years of such employment. If the degree is earned while the family member is in the full-time employ of the company, he or she will be reimbursed for tuition and related costs for each term in which a B average or better is received. Family members who become permanent employees and already have master's degrees in business or topics directly related to our business will be paid a bonus of $20,000 to be divided into equal quarterly installments over the first four years of employment.

As a condition of continued employment after receiving a master's degree, a family member must complete sixty hours of approved continuing professional education in each calendar year. Failure to do so will freeze the family member's salary for one year and jeopardize his or her employment status.

Redefinition of Relationships

New boundaries, structures, and policies change how family members relate to one another in and out of the business and how they relate to outside advisors and senior managers. Advisors should anticipate and understand such changes.

Relationships with Outside Advisors. As the business puts the new mediating structures in place, the scope of influence and the relationship of the company advisor, accountant, banker, and others will need to be redefined. For instance, after a financial expert joins a board of directors, the accountant who was part of the company's inner circle and provided strategic financial advice will likely move to a more perfunctory role, perhaps limited to the auditing and annual reporting. It is also possible that an advisor might move into a more intense relationship with the board.

We believe that professional advisors should consider how their resources can best be used to serve the client. A board with several outside directors provides a team of resources that far exceeds any individual's advice. However, it is a conflict of interest for existing advisors to continue as advisor and serve as director of a board. Membership on the board should be based on competence in areas of critical importance to the business and not on friendship or other links with the owner.

Relationships with Senior Management. The owners need to direct the efforts of a team of senior managers to make the company successful. In most family businesses, one member of the senior management team—such as the president of the company—is also a member of the board of directors. This potential confusion of boundaries may cause conflict and should be addressed in some of the documentation on roles and responsibilities. Owners should hold senior managers accountable for the success of the business and provide guidance and direction as needed. The established structures, such as boards of directors and family forums, and policies should also help clarify when family members who serve in more than one role are wearing one hat or the other.

Summary

Each family business is different and calls for a unique approach. However, clear structures and policies are always needed.

Setbacks and rough going—especially in the beginning—are inevitable. Furthermore, establishing these structures is a lengthy process. It is likely to take twelve to eighteen months to get mediating structures up and running and to get all parties to feel comfortable and understand the structures' purpose and how to make them work for them. The key for family business advisors is to be persistent, maintain a positive focus, and trust the process.

1. Determine a way to separate family and business issues and structure the interface of the two systems to work effectively.

2. In most situations, consider the family business system to be your client. As we mentioned in Chapter One, defining the client as only one or two stakeholders among the many not only shortchange the possibilities for a more elegant solution, it may also sow the seeds of dissension and failure in the future.

3. Encourage the family to develop employment and financial distribution policies, mission statements and such. The development of these understandings will enhance team building and focus the family in a positive direction. Committing these to writing imbues them with more meaning and power and will enable stakeholders to refer to them during future conflicts.

4. Maintain a balanced perspective and work to achieve success on all fronts using multiple agendas. Recognize that the task is complex and that your success will require a commitment to this complexity and the skill to work within it. Should the professional find that he cannot function in this manner, then he may wish to consider incorporating a family business consultant into the teamwork, so that the goals of the client can best be achieved.

Part Three

Common Problems,
Uncommon Solutions

This part examines three of the most common areas in which professional advisors work: succession, wealth management, and estate planning. We do not offer suggestions for expert practice in these areas but rather offer a family systems perspective of each. Our intention is to help professionals add some process consulting tools to their professional practice in these areas.

Chapter Eight looks at the most common and most difficult problem family businesses face: generational succession in ownership and management. Families need to begin early to plan and consider this transition. The chapter explains how the professional can help the family take a deeper look at the meaning of this shift of generations, authority, and resources. In Chapter Nine we look at an important issue for families in business that is not often discussed: learning to handle wealth. We offer some ideas and suggestions that financial advisors can integrate into a discussion about the impact of inheritance and family wealth on individuals. Finally, in Chapter Ten we examine estate-planning issues in the context of the family systems perspective.

Common Problems, Common Solutions

Chapter Eight

Establishing Succession in Ownership and Leadership

Whatever issues, problems, or tasks your family business client has called you to tackle, the presence—or absence—of a business succession plan will greatly affect your work. In addition, no matter your area of expertise as an advisor, you will play a critical role in generational succession and the transfer of control.

The most dangerous period a business faces is that of succession, when ownership and leadership pass from one person to another. In a family business, especially one moving from first to second generation, the shift is often from one person to several and a challenge for both the family and the business. We estimate that as many as 85 percent of the crises a family business faces arise around the issues of succession.

Ownership and leadership of a business can pass to members of the next generation, representatives of that generation, or outside agents. The challenge for professional advisors is to help the family see that succession is not simply a business decision, a financial decision, or a family decision but a process that must take place over many years, involving family, business, and financial choices and often necessitating a delicate balancing act. This chapter will guide you through some of the common dilemmas and choices that your family business client will have to make.

The accountant guides the valuation process that determines the price per share. The banker provides some of the funds to effect the transfer of the shares. The estate planner takes a comprehensive, long-term view of the development of a strategy that effects the transfer, minimizes the tax consequences, and may incorporate features for children, grandchildren, and as-yet-unborn descendants. The insurance underwriter helps manage uncertainty by brokering any insurance that is part of the plan, making certain that the ownership of the insurance is properly placed either inside or outside an estate or owned by the company and that the insurance is purchased at the right rate.

One or more of these advisors may have been instrumental in creating irrevocable trusts to which family members are beneficiaries or charitable trusts that are operated by the family but benefit the community or special causes. One or more of these advisors may also be a trustee for one of these trusts.

Teamwork

The client is best served when all advisors work as a team to complete and implement the details of a succession plan. Any one of them can initiate the team concept with the client, perhaps by asking the client to call a meeting of all advisors.

Even advisors who are not experts in succession planning should be knowledgeable enough about the topic to spot problems with existing plans and initiate discussions with owners and potential successors about the issues they will need to confront.

Advisors have two tasks in the succession process. First, they must help the client see the situation in a broad context. Second, they may need to shift their role from problem solver to coach, teaching the client to solve the problem alone. The choices of business ownership, leadership, and succession cannot be delegated to outside professionals, although professionals can guide clients through the process and share their experiences.

A good place to start is by helping clients develop a clear picture of what things will look like after the business transfer is complete. These are some of the questions that may be explored:

- What will the financial profile of the retiring owner be?

- What plan can best assure the ongoing financial stability of the enterprise?
- What governing structure will exist in the business?
- What qualifications must the successor have?
- Who are the candidates for successor?
- What special provisions must be made for children who may eventually own company stock?
- What specific plans must be made to effect the full and complete transfer to the successor?

Advisors will customize these questions according to their discipline. It may be productive for each in the team of advisors to serve as primary advisor on a rotating basis in order to elicit a diversity of perspectives. It is important to keep the focus and momentum going until the succession plan is finalized, documented, made legal, and properly funded.

In the next sections we present some general problems that often prevent succession plans from being implemented. We go on to explore the challenges of succession and how the family can plan for its outcome. Finally, we look at the options and methods of selling the business, an alternative that is a good choice for some families.

When to Begin Planning

Many people mistakenly believe that succession is an event that occurs when the business owner is ready to retire. In reality, succession is a process that begins when potential successors are still children. It is during this period that parents teach their children important attitudes about people, work, money, competence, quality, confidence, the work ethic, life balance, and commitments. They set the stage for children to grow and find a life's work that will bring them satisfaction. They also should set the stage for a smooth transition by helping their children develop into capable future leaders and by crafting plans and documents that will enable the business to survive periods of turbulence and crisis.

As Figure 8.1 illustrates, succession is marked by a shift of power and influence and a period of shared power.

It is never too early to put a succession plan in place. Accidents happen; premature death occurs. Responsible business owners who have concern for the continuity of the enterprise and the well-being of their heirs will welcome advisors assisting in this all-important task. Unfortunately, many owners find it difficult to grapple with the emotional and financial issues that succession planning requires.

Many businesses began during the economic expansion period following World War II. Their founders are now reaching or have reached the age at which they must question what to do with the business they spent so many years building. Their children may be wondering when their parents will hand over the reins.

Figure 8.1. Shifting and Sharing of Power and Influence.

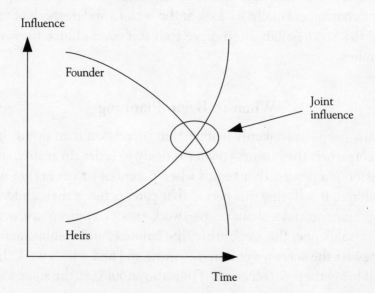

Businesses that began with entrepreneurial zeal are often dominated by the sheer force of their founders. It is not unusual for a business to be built on the unique skills, insights, understanding, and passion of the founder. If that person exits the picture without proper planning, a hole is created that may be difficult to fill.

In contrast, some owners never leave. One CEO's fifty-something son reported that his eighty-five-year-old father had finally let go of the company's everyday affairs. The reason: he was going on his honeymoon! The third generation was not interested in the business so preparations were made to sell it. The CEO was glad his grandchildren had found other careers. He believed the family business had been a form of slavery for him.

Another business had a different problem. Rick was always the golden boy and heir apparent to his father, the chairman of the family's financial services company. After earning a master's degree in business Rick spent three years with a large investment bank in New York. He then entered the company and began to work alongside his father, who had inherited the business from his own father. Dad, age fifty, was planning retirement. Still Rick was itching to make his mark. After seven years, a large company offered Rick a division presidency. Rick decided to take it and told his father so. The next week the board voted to make Rick president. He stayed. However, like many heirs, he found he had responsibility without authority. Again he felt he wanted to withdraw. Dad had difficulty listening to Rick. He had waited for his own father to retire and assumed that Rick would do the same. Also, like many people in their late fifties, he wanted to consolidate the business and ensure his own future. In addition, his entrepreneurial energy was low whereas Rick was eager to move into new markets and take advantage of some opportunities he had spotted.

A consultant was hired to help with a succession planning process and decisions about how to accomplish the transition. After several talks father and son saw that their value differences had to do with their respective stages in life. Dad agreed to a more limited role overseeing investment opportunities with some of the firm's long-term clients. He purchased another small business so that he could let go of this one without actually retiring. Rick began to run the business.

Women have more opportunity in enlightened family enterprises than they do in publicly held companies. Evidence of the glass ceiling is supported by the fact that very few of the Fortune 500 companies are headed by women. Additionally, many capable daughters, wives, and granddaughters have not been allowed to make significant contributions to the family business because of unquestioned traditions about women and the family business: "A woman's place is in the home." "We need leaders who will make a full-time commitment to a career in the business but she'll want to leave when she gets married and has babies." "What does she know about finance?"

Professionally run companies base employment decisions on objective criteria. They must also base their examination of potential successors on competence, training, and desire to revitalize the company and assure its continuity. This procedure is in stark contrast to the archaic method of primogeniture. There is no evidence that the firstborn male in any generation is genetically wired to be the best business leader.

Advisors should start by exploring several basic questions:

- Should the business be sold or should it go forward?
- If it is sold what will happen to family members?
- If it goes forward, what is required to make the transition successful?
- How much change is required in either the way the family runs the business or the business itself?
- What is the best way to accomplish these changes?
- What personal factors are involved?
- What business factors are involved?

- How capable is the family of making these changes?
- What are the sources of resistance to change?

Overcoming Resistance

Some founders deny the necessity for succession planning. They say, "They will have to carry me out of here." At some point they are indeed carried out and the family is left to pick up the pieces. These founders increase the risk that their business will fail after they have left it because they have not prepared either the business or the people in it for management and ownership.

Founders are understandably reluctant to confront the issues of succession. Parents may fear that succession planning will force them to choose one child from several as successor and create conflict that will destroy the family. The children may view this choice as a referendum on which one their parents love most. Some parents may question whether the heir apparent can do the job. For their part, succession planning forces children to confront their own capabilities and desires. It also tends to drag up old sibling rivalries and other unresolved family issues.

Because the process is often an emotional rather than a rational one, it may seem to the founder and his wife that it is easier just to avoid the whole thing. Most family business management is informal. The family often never learns to do systematic planning together. Also, many family members do not work in other business organizations before joining the family business and have not been exposed to or trained in traditional business planning. Family members who attempt planning without these skills often get caught up in personal issues; conversations deteriorate into arguments, and the result is a stalemate.

Over the years the founder may have adopted a mode of running the business that isolated and insulated him from the succession issue. For a long time, perhaps, he has been the one upon whom everyone else depended. He has made the hard decisions and shouldered all responsibilities. Over time—and by necessity—he has come to rely primarily on his own judgment.

This was the case with Jerry Linden, sixty-eight, who had founded a single-location country-style restaurant that had succeeded beyond his wildest dreams. His son and daughter, in their early forties, were capable, shrewd, and hardworking. Yet despite his confidence in their ability to manage Jerry kept putting off transferring control. Two things stood in the way: Jerry's largest emotional and financial assets were represented by the business.

Jerry's life revolved around his business. It had even become his dinner table, with most of his meals taken at a choice table in the dining room. Like many entrepreneurs, Jerry didn't know what he would do with his time if he retired. Although he had acquired a good amount of real estate over the years, the business remained his largest single asset. He had not funded his retirement program; rather, his retirement income was tied to the ongoing operation of the business. (When owners set things up this way they feel they are still in the business even after transfer of ownership and management. They tend to be uncomfortable about the way the business is operated and often meddle in the affairs of the company.)

Any of Jerry's advisors could have initiated a planning process to address the succession and retirement issues by doing the following:

- Pushing to see that retirement funds were set aside
- Helping the successors purchase directly their father's shares with the inclusion of a deferred compensation package to give Jerry a lump sum payment and continued income for the life of the package

These actions were finally taken. But Jerry still had to deal with his second concern—time. His real estate was an opportunity to stay active. The lump sum payment he had received enabled him to develop his land. One large parcel he owned was a farm along the state highway that moved through town. The farm contained some beautiful, historic buildings and the original early Victorian farmhouse. Ever the entrepreneur, Jerry arranged to have a portion of the farm zoned for housing and used the area around the farm buildings and house to build a historic village, with antique stores, a blacksmith's shop, a country store, and other shops. In this case, Jerry's passion for the new venture enabled him to let go and let his children run his original business.

Developing a Plan

Developing a smart succession plan is not easy. It takes time. The payoff is that building a business over the course of a lifetime and then successfully passing it on to one's children can be an enormously satisfying experience.

The following six steps constitute a rough outline of the bases for advisors to cover in order to achieve successful succession planning.

Step One: Get a commitment from all family members—founder included—to work on succession planning. A commitment means committing the necessary time and financial resources. Family members also must be patient, open-minded, and willing to compromise self-interest for the good of the group. The touchstone of the commitment is the realization of the consequences for family members—both financially and personally—of failure to achieve successful planning.

Step Two: Help family members set aside competitive ways and teach them more constructive ways to work together. It is critical that the adversarial tone that characterizes many sibling relations be minimized. These feelings will probably never be overcome completely but if the family can't learn to deal with them, ultimately someone will want to be bought out.

Step Three: Adopt a business planning process that begins with a mission statement and strategic plan. Developing a mission statement for the family and another one for the business are the first steps to being more systematic about the future direction of the business and the family. (See Chapter Five for more on this.) In addition, top managers should institutionalize the business's formula for success to decrease its dependency on the founder. Their goal should be to run the business efficiently and effectively while maintaining the special qualities that originally made the business successful.

Step Four: Create a personal development plan for family members who work in the business. A personal development plan strives to nurture the skills necessary for individuals to be successful when they continue to develop the business. The family business advisor should emphasize that personal goals and personal development will improve the business and give everyone a clear understanding of the overall direction of the company and how each individual fits into it.

Accountants can initiate a process to educate family members, both in and out of the business, about the company finances. The single most common shortcoming of the successor group is failure to understand fully the financial aspects of the company. Advisors of all stripes can recommend that potential successors better prepare themselves by taking business courses at the local community college and attending conferences, seminars, and workshops offered by their industry's trade association.

Step Five: Develop an appropriate governance structure for the ownership-management interface of the business. A family board (or board of directors for larger companies) and a family forum can balance the diverse interests of all players in a way that works for the business, for the family, and for each individual. (See Chapter Seven for more on these structures.) They provide a forum to create policy and debate business and family concerns and a formal board to make and oversee business decisions.

Step Six: Put in place legal and financial structures to implement the succession plan. Many founders try to make the business plan fit the estate plan when in fact the two should be developed simultaneously. Even the best estate plan may simply be unworkable for the succession of a business or may generate very bad feelings between family members. A common mistake is to leave equal amounts of stock to those children who work in the business and those who do not.

From One to Several

The overarching concept that advisors often need to help owners understand is that the succession shift is not just from one owner to the next but from one person to many. Even in second-generation family businesses where one heir is selected as the business leader, ownership is most often shared among several heirs, usually siblings.

When there is shared power or authority the governing structures are especially critical. There must be clear boundaries, expectations, and relationships between the family board or forum and the business. A family that asks for help in making a succession plan or a succession decision often really needs help in creating the mediating governance structures that will enable the business to operate and help them share the different levels of policy making and decision making.

Following the six-step process requires families to step back, look at a broader picture of the issues, and make several shifts in their thinking and methods of interaction. As we already noted, they need to be willing to invest significant time and to include all family members in the process. They also need to realize that the outcome will emerge from a process that leads to change rather than from a single decision or event.

Family and business authority can be conceptualized as a part of a continuum, as Figure 8.2 illustrates.

In a family, especially when there are several children, the most appropriate governing method is a democratic one. Businesses tend to be governed more autocratically, although the two systems should

Figure 8.2. Family Versus Business Governing Methods.

Democracy ◄──────────────────────► Autocracy

not be governed at opposite ends of the pole. The distinctions in governing methods need to be made explicit and the boundary line between family and business clearly defined.

In the process of succession, the family will most likely have to call in the services of one or more professional advisors who will assess several dimensions of the business.

- The pool of potential heirs and their relationships to the business, what they want from it, and what they can offer
- The business's needs and strategy for the future
- The desires and wishes of current business owners and leaders
- The various options that may be pursued, including modes of bequeathing the business and possible sale to an outside party

Transferring Control to Family Members

Transferring a business to the next generation can be a rewarding experience because both current and prospective owners and managers are, at least theoretically, in it together despite different needs, hopes, and goals. Advisors should look for opportunities to identify and opportunities to change the negative patterns and emotions that can break a succession plan.

Resistance to Letting Go

When the company is sold, the exiting owners may hold collateral in the business. Certain contractual provisions may tie their retirement income to the company's future cash flow. The children, especially those who have not been actively involved in the business or who have a domineering parent may not feel as if the stock is really theirs. It takes a while for such children to feel they are the rightful owners of a business, sometimes as long as two years. If during that time they need to make decisions that affect the value of the stock they find it hard to participate fully in the process.

When parents gift their business to children, they really do give up control. Still, they may be tempted to undermine the children—for instance, directing longtime nonfamily executives to make certain decisions.

The role of the exiting owner needs to be clearly delineated. An advisor should also be sensitive to signals that a founder is progressing through different emotional stages and be alert for any signs of depression.

Evaluating the Business's Ability to Support the Transaction

A buyout increases the company's debt—usually by a large factor—putting the balance sheet in disarray and increasing the firm's interest expense. Often payments come out of future earnings, which can starve the company for capital. Some transactions are structured to require an underperforming or nonperforming business to be a kind of leveraged race car. A healthy transaction creates a legal and financial framework that doesn't impose unrealistic expectations or restraints on new ownership and management.

Owners often have a hard time coming to grips with how much money they need to support their lifestyles and committing themselves to the process of reducing the value of their estate for tax purposes. Some parents prefer to continue to build net worth in their estate, not trusting their children to provide for them. Ideally, when parents sell stock to children by way of an installment note, they freeze the value of the stock at current value. Often the note is interest only, which keeps the payments low but preserves the parents' cash flow. When parents die, children inherit the note at the frozen value, even if the business has grown and the value increased by then.

Calculating a Realistic Value of the Business

There are many legitimate ways to determine a business's value. Usually, family members work hard to prove the business is worth very little for tax purposes—until it is time to sell. The fair market value may be a point of contention in the family. For instance, one client applied a 50 percent discount to the estimated fair market value for estate planning purposes. This man didn't realize that when his children wanted to sell stock to make a down payment on a house or pay a tuition bill, they would have to transfer their stock using the same valuation formula.

If transactions such as gifts to children or charitable donations involving stock were based on a discounted value it may be difficult to prove to the IRS that the business's value has suddenly soared. Owners often hire an outside business appraiser only to toss the estimate received because they believe it is unrealistically low.

Protecting Exiting Owners from Deteriorating Assets

If parents sell the business to their children through an installment note, the note should include covenants similar to those a bank requires before making a similar loan, including limits on net worth and borrowing and contingencies for possible foreclosure or default of the loan. An independent group, much like a board or loan committee, can monitor performance of the loan and the company.

Understanding the Issues of Group Control

Many parents underestimate the problems that a transfer from one person to many people can create and do not understand the issues and challenges that must be addressed for the process to be successful. Once the decision-making process is divided among several people decisions can be endlessly delayed by inertia or controversy. When a company run "by committee" does make a decision, it may be made to appease rather than to meet objective business criteria. If the group has no history or skills in working together, the advisor can encourage it to go through a process of team building, developing ground rules for working together.

Selling to a Third Party

The decision to sell a family business should be based on several factors, including the following: Are there competent successors who are willing to run the business? Can the business sustain the financial needs of a growing family? Is there a market for the business at a price that will satisfy current owners? Does the business need a capital infusion to survive?

Selling the business does not represent a failure. A sale can be a financially and emotionally rewarding decision. Perpetuating family ownership, even of a multigeneration business, when family members don't want it or are not competent to run it doesn't make sense and may even devaluate the company. One litmus test is comparing the business's return on equity with returns the family could achieve in other investments.

However, even if it makes financial sense to sell the business doing so may be a difficult process. Advisors may have to help the family confront many difficult issues.

Sale of a Legacy

Often the family sees selling a business as a deeply emotional and personal issue—sort of like selling Grandma. This kind of feeling is very common and it complicates the decision-making process. If emotional issues are not understood and acknowledged, they can surface as hidden resistance and undermine negotiations even when the family is acting as if it is ready to sell the business. Individuals may argue fine points, not respond to questions, and refuse to share information. In any sale process, it is imperative that the individual responsibilities are clearly focused. Someone has to be head honcho in charge of negotiations. A committee to sell the business is not needed but the family should designate a small subgroup to lead the process. If emotional issues are allowed to rule the deliberations, the family risks missing a critical opportunity. The business's asset value may be reduced because buyers understand the family's vulnerabilities and fragment the selling group. This is more likely to happen when different factions have different expectations that put them at cross-purposes.

In the early stages of a business, the owners must produce a product or service in order to win a place in the market. Although owners continue to pursue excellence in that area, after a certain level of performance, the conceptual business changes even when the fundamental business remains the same. The larger and more stable a business becomes, the more it becomes a matter of asset management. Every business is comprised of a pool of assets—property, buildings, and equipment—which, by producing a product or service, create sales and profits that relate to the asset base.

The Marzotto family, a well-recognized name in business in Italy, is a good example of this concept. The Marzottos have been in business for more than four hundred years. Once sword manufacturers, today the family owns Marzotto Textiles, a men's clothing line that bears that name, as well as Hugo Boss, Jolli Hotels, and many other businesses. Over the years the family has been in many different lines of work. When each business opportunity was fully exploited, the family sold it and repositioned its assets in another. The family has bought and sold and bought and sold, all the while compounding its asset base. This strategy has moved the family away from the notion that the business is a monument to the founder or his family. All the members of the Marzotto family know what business they are really in: increasing the family's financial asset base.

Financial and legal advisors to family businesses can do a real service by helping owners and their families see the wisdom of the Marzotto viewpoint, the long view of the family business that spans generations. To do this, advisors can follow some guidelines. First, they should try to get the family to talk openly together about the emotional and personal meaning of the sale. If the advisor is unaware of these issues, they will trip the advisor up. The advisor can help the family see that their feelings are not wrong or bad but need to be taken into account. Second, advisors should help clarify the difference between the family's emotional reactions and the business decisions. If they cannot separate the two, they will not be able to conduct their business prudently. They need to be aware of the emotions but make objective business decisions. Third, if the family decides not to sell based on personal and emotional grounds, the advisor should make sure that everyone takes responsibility for that decision and understands its consequences. If they do not, the risk is that the family or even the advisor may later be taken to task for the negative consequences of a decision the family has made.

The Impact on the Children

New owners may want to streamline payroll by stripping out some family salaries. Many family businesses overcompensate family members, who then have a tough time earning as much on the open market. If they have worked nowhere but in the family business, they may not find another job easily. Children also may feel disappointed or resentful if they are not given a chance to prove themselves by running the business.

Unsophisticated Sellers

A common mistake occurs when owners expect the transaction to go smoothly. How well the owners have kept up with financial reporting will determine if they have the right financial information to present to potential buyers. They may have no idea of the impact that due diligence will have on the business. Due diligence is like an audit; owners may not be comfortable providing all the information a buyer requires. Advisors should prepare owners for this necessary part of the transaction.

Legal and Investment Banking Professionals

Owners may be unpleasantly surprised when they discover how steep the fees for the necessary legal and investment banking services can be, but advisors would be wise to make owners aware of the consequences of not having appropriate help. They should point out that although these fees may seem high they will represent only a small percentage of the proceeds from the sale.

A family who owned a grocery with $100 million in annual sales received an offer of $4 million to sell the business. The owners decided to do so without the help of an investment banker, whose significant fee would have come to more than a year's worth of gross revenue. As they were structuring the deal, another offer for twice as much came over the transom. The first bidder threatened to sue if the owner did not pursue the original bid so the family turned down the second offer and ended up with a deal that failed to protect adequately the outgoing owners from the future financial health of the business. Three years later, the company went out of business and the family's payments were subjugated to bankruptcy, resulting in only a fraction of what they expected to receive. One fifty-year-old son who had continued to work for the new owners was out on the street. All of this could have been avoided if the family had hired necessary professionals!

A Reasonable—and Acceptable—Value

Especially when selling to an outsider, owners expect to factor into the price all the sacrifices they have made and guilt they have felt for not being more available to their families. The business's value becomes the answer to the question, "Why did you work so hard?" The owners may overprice their company in an effort to try to support a comfortable retirement. Overpricing can also be an unconscious way to sabotage a sale. An owner may honestly believe that he or she wants to sell but end up claiming, "I tried to sell the business but no one would give me what it is worth." Indeed, many owners hire a professional appraiser only to find they don't like the value offered and disregard it.

Information Leaks

Many owners underestimate or ignore the degree to which information about a possible sale can leak out and do damage. For instance, if longtime employees hear rumors of a sale they will worry about how it will affect them. They may feel that the family is selling out and deserting them. Morale and productively may slip, making the company less marketable.

Advisors can help prepare owners to anticipate such concerns and address them. They can also help owners manage the flow of information to employees and the community and decide thoughtfully what to say and how to say it so that people are informed as the process unfolds.

The Emotional Impact

Most families have no idea of the confusion and distraction that they, their employees, and their customers are bound to experience. Family business members will need to juggle several strategies simultaneously: they will have to run the business as if they plan to be there forever even while they negotiate its sale.

Economic Realities

Many owners have only the most limited notion of the tax implications of selling a business and the actual proceeds from a sale. Walking a family through different financial scenarios not only prepares owners but also serves to test how they feel about the transaction before making the plunge. If their motivation for selling the business is to get a wheelbarrow full of money and they realize they will end up with only half a wheelbarrow, they may not be able to decide to proceed before investing substantial time and resources.

Estate Planning Goals

Finally, the family should be aware that they may be able to structure the sale in a way that enhances estate planning goals. If an advisor is not able to provide that information, he or she may be able to help the family find an expert who can.

Summary

In this chapter we looked at the processes that make up the most important event a family business will face: transfer of power from the founder to a new generation. The difficulty of doing this is compounded when the people making the shift are members of the same family and when some of the bystanders to the process have an investment in its outcome.

The chapter offered some tools and techniques for advisors to use to help families change their view of succession from a single event to a process. Advisors usually work longer on issues of succession with a family business than on any other kinds of issues. This is because the challenges of succession cannot be resolved during a single retreat or gathering or in a single agreement but rather must evolve over time.

Continuity of the business, maintenance or improvement of market position, and stability of the workforce are all signs that a successful transfer of control has been achieved.

Chapter Nine

Managing Inherited Wealth

When you work with a family that has substantial wealth, it is important to observe the way they handle it to make sure it is not a disincentive for them to lead productive lives. Most people define themselves through their activities. People who have enough money to make work an option still need some activities to give their lives meaning.

Advisors are well positioned to influence the family's attitudes about their wealth. Doing so is part of the theme we emphasize in this book: helping family business members function responsibly within the family and the business systems. In Chapter Seven we discussed the creation of family forums that teach money management and develop policies to encourage individual competence. In this chapter we explore how advisors can help clients make wise choices about their money and teach their children to do the same.

The meaning of wealth encompasses what it offers individuals and how they expect to use it. Differences in perspectives can ignite conflicts. A family fortune is a livelihood, a measurement of success, a conspicuous emblem of status, a source of identity, and a burden. Money may be equated with love, preference, trust, maturity, values, and respect.

Professionals who serve families and their enterprises often find themselves in the inner circle as the family makes important financial decisions. If a trust is to be drawn, the client may ask the advisor about how it should be structured. When a will is drafted, the advisor may be called in to draft provisions that will protect younger children and perhaps others. As an estate begins to accumulate, advisors may be able to advise how best to prepare the family. These are just some opportunities advisors have to initiate a proactive stance that ensures that all stakeholder interests are served.

An advisor working with a family must learn not just the ways in which family members wish to dispose of their wealth but also the money's meaning for each person. In some cases, preparations for and expectations about substantial wealth can be a burden rather than a benefit.

This chapter looks at some of the ways that advisors can help family business clients explore the personal meaning of their wealth and guide them to create specific plans for wealth preservation and inheritance.

The Personal Dilemmas of Wealth

Here are some examples of the personal dilemmas that family money can pose for different family members:

- One twenty-seven-year-old son of a very successful family business owner declared, "It is ridiculous that an eighteen-hundred-square-foot apartment in an unfinished building costs one point two million dollars. It is also ridiculous that it costs six hundred fifty thousand dollars to finish the apartment. What is really ridiculous is that I, at twenty-seven years of age, just wrote the check to pay for it all!" Later, during a discussion of the impact of his wealth the same young man announced, "I am not my money!"

- In another family, the father died young, leaving his twenty-four-year-old son in absolute control of a $30 million estate. The son was a student at a university on the East Coast who frequently liked to visit his family in the Southwest. It took substantial discussion to convince him that it would be inappropriate for him to buy his own Lear jet.

- Another young man, who had led a sheltered childhood, went away to college and began to gain a larger perspective. When he returned home for a visit he asked his mother, "Are we rich?" "Yes," she said, after a long and obviously painful pause. "Why didn't you and Dad tell me?" the son asked.

Such stories illustrate that considerable confusion often surrounds wealth. It makes little difference if it is new money or old money, inherited or freshly earned. Wealth may still be confusing. Some individuals spend the bulk of their careers amassing a substantial fortune and then the rest of their lives obsessed with protecting it from the tax man and from children who might become spendthrifts. They worry about people taking advantage of them. Some are so afraid of losing their wealth that they hoard every penny. Indeed, the matter was so confusing to one group of people that they formed a support group—called the Dough-Nuts—that has the express purpose of providing a forum where wealthy people can discuss their feelings and attitudes about their wealth.

A family's attitude about wealth colors their approach to whatever issues an advisor is called in to address. Helping them sort through these attitudes can help the advisor clarify and resolve other presenting problems.

Helping Young People Deal with Wealth

Few people realize that there is a real stigma—perhaps even a prejudice—about people with wealth in our society. This prejudice causes some wealthy persons to deny their wealth. In effect they put up an imaginary screen between themselves and others. Unfortunately, this screen is quite visible and creates a barrier to sound interpersonal relationships.

One wealthy family is waging a battle with the state over a narrow strip of abandoned land that, more than a hundred years ago, was a roadway between their homes and the ocean. There have been two previous attempts to resolve the matter, one in 1964 and one in 1968, each with conflicting rulings. The dispute has heated up again and sides are being taken. The homeowners have sought mediation and want a win-win solution, one that balances the interests of the state with those of the family. The local headlines read, "Wealthy homeowners attempt to buy the beach!" This is a clear distortion of fact. In a guest editorial one of the homeowners reminded readers, "Even wealthy people are entitled to due process!" The family members, young and old, feel that they are being unfairly persecuted in the press and discriminated against. In this case their wealth clearly sets them apart from others. They are the victims of what we call *wealth prejudice*.

Indeed, wealth prejudice is a common phenomenon. It is the job of parents to help children understand the opportunity, obligations, and responsibilities that go with wealth and prepare them to deal with the challenges that will come to them in the world.

Family wealth can be very confusing to children. In grammar school children say things that are hurtful. A ten-year-old told of being taunted on the playground by classmates chanting, "You're rich!" The boy didn't know what to say. He knew that his family had had much opportunity but nothing in his upbringing had prepared him for such an experience. He responded by saying, "No I'm not!" Thus he learned to lie to gain acceptance.

What begins in grammar school continues. Emily French was a sophomore at a large university. Her father and grandfather had given the funds to build the large dormitory named French Hall. One of Emily's classmates asked, "French Hall—is that any relation to you?" Emily felt embarrassed and didn't know what to say. Finally she blurted out that there was a family connection.

Emily's brother, Brad, had a different concern. He was an affable, humble, and handsome young man with many interests. But he often feared he was liked or sought after just because of his wealth rather than because of his personality or talents.

Family business advisors in most professions can help young family members deal with the issues surrounding wealth by teaching confidentiality, encouraging members to lead productive lives, and teaching fiscal responsibility and independent money management.

Teaching Confidentiality

Knowing how to handle confidential information about family financial status is the underlying theme of these stories. Some families are reluctant to discuss the family wealth for fear of the information falling into the wrong hands. Parents may say, "What they don't know won't hurt them."

Confidentiality is built on trust. Children need to learn early on that some matters are private family issues that are not for discussion with persons outside the family.

One Example of the Learning Process

One family business consultant began working with a wealthy family composed of a mother, a father, and six children ages twelve through twenty-three. The parents had launched an education program with one of the objectives being to educate the children in such a manner that wealth would not have a deleterious impact on them.

The advisor designed a comprehensive education program for the family that centered on the study of the Anasazi Indians of the Southwest. The purpose was to place the family in a sparse environment where they could see for themselves how a culture can create, love, educate, and pass along meaning for future generations.

The program began at the Crow Canyon Archeological Center in Cortez, Colorado. In a private exhibit arranged for the family, the Crow Canyon curators had arranged artifacts and other pieces of information on seven tables with each table representing an evolutionary stage of these people whose history spanned the period from 10,000 B.C. to A.D. 1350. The family was divided into two teams. Each was given the task of identifying the artifacts and their purpose and then listing the seven tables in sequence from oldest to newest. Doing so required discussion of how the Anasazi had lived, how they had maintained themselves, and the challenges they had faced. This exercise was followed by hands-on experience of some of the tasks the Anasazi did, such as starting a fire by using friction or using an atlatl (a device for throwing a spear or a dart). The family sat in a replica of a pit house and talked about how life would have been for those who really lived there. It was interesting to watch the children's reaction as they learned that two of them would have died from the early childhood illnesses they'd had, had they been Anasazi children; that their father and mother would have died already, as they had substantially passed the Anasazi life expectancy; and that their teenage sisters would have already been mothers several times over!

The next day an archeological guide took the group to a remote canyon that contained extensive unexcavated Anasazi ruins. Along the five-mile hike they found pottery shards, pictographs, and petroglyphs on canyon walls, and small kivas. Back in their own rooms at the end of the day the group discussed the experience. They wrote down their individual thoughts on what could be learned from the "Ancient Ones."

To many readers, taking a family into the wilderness to come to an understanding about survival and the strength of family ties may seem a bit of a stretch. But sometimes it is efficacious to sever wealthy family systems from their secure settings in order to allow them to consider poignant questions about the basics of life. When all the assumed boundaries are made invisible individuals are forced to come up with a new set of rules.

The study of the ancients was relevant to this family. The children learned that the ancients had educated their children out of love and because they wanted to perpetuate the culture. Similarly, their parents were trying to educate them in the areas relevant to their lives. Most important, they learned that their parents cared about them and wanted to keep the family entity ongoing.

The whole family learned that they must do the same as the ancients had to survive as a family—the parents had to teach, the children had to listen, and all had to use all of their skills. They learned that there is strength in numbers. A team is a formidable unit. Sticking together would help them accomplish their goals. Dependence on other family members was an asset. Creativity would come out of this dependence.

After a discussion in which these ideas were raised, the family talked about the problems they confronted because of their wealth. The issue of confidentiality came up immediately. It was decided that the family should create their own definitions of confidentiality in order to create a working basis for dealing with the issue as a group and as individuals.

Defining Confidentiality

The following are definitions of confidentiality created by different families.

- Some things are private.
- Confidentiality involves things told to you that are meant to stay within the group, the family, or between individuals.
- Confidentiality means privileged information. Anyone else is not to know about it.
- Confidentiality involves the ability to have trust in a person or persons that certain conversations or feelings will be kept as private knowledge.
- Confidentiality is based on a trust that is maintained. If that trust is broken, so is the confidentiality.
- Confidentiality involves sharing information that will never be used in a hurtful way.

In earlier chapters of this book we discussed the concept of boundaries between such matters as ownership and career opportunity. The matter of boundaries comes up once again in the confidentiality issue. Here the boundaries are about what information is appropriate for all people, family and nonfamily members, to have.

Although it was too late to help Emily French respond to that first inquiry about French Hall, the family business advisor helped her parents prepare her should she be asked that question again. She was coached and rehearsed her response so it would be direct, straightforward, and honest. To all further questions, she was likely to reply as follows: "Yes, that building was given to the university by my father and grandfather. They both work very hard and have been financially successful in their business. They believe it is important to contribute and give back to such institutions as our church, the university, and many different causes in our community. I'm very proud of my family for doing it and I hope I will be able to carry that tradition on in the future." Emily would never again feel guilty or flustered when confronted with that aspect of the family wealth.

Let us analyze what was done and relate it to the concept of boundaries. First, Emily was informed that other donations were in progress. Her parents no longer took the what-she-doesn't-know-won't-hurt-her point of view. The family and their advisor discussed the family values of giving and how such gifts were likely to occur in the future. Emily and her siblings would be involved in the discussions. As they matured, it was likely that they would take active roles in the process. Instead of apologizing for the family wealth, Emily learned to speak the truth about it, thus reinforcing a positive image of herself and her family. She was also practicing one of her family's values, namely, educating others. Emily was also prepared for follow-up questions such as "How did your father and grandfather make their money?" or "What other charities does your family contribute to?" Should someone be so crass as to ask "How much money does your family have?" Emily even learned the kind of answer she could give: a partial answer, saying politely, "I understand your curiosity but we have an agreement in our family that the subject is only discussed within the family."

Encouraging Individuals to Lead Productive Lives

The way in which parents think about and handle their wealth offers a good indication of how the children's views will develop.

Family Charter

One wealthy family was so concerned about conveying a clear message that they created a family charter that detailed their expectations, values, and rules about their wealth and inheritance. Part of the charter read as follows:

> We are a family committed to our members and descendants being responsible, productive, well-educated citizens who practice the work ethic and make constructive contributions in the local community and the world at large. Each member is encouraged to develop and use self-supporting, marketable skills that contribute to the enhancement of his or her own self-esteem and independence.

This family clearly recognized the importance of self-esteem and subscribed to the notion that having financial resources should not be a disincentive for constructive contributions. Advisors can suggest that their family business clients take time to sort through their own values, expectations, and rules about wealth as the basis for their own family charters.

As we travel the world and meet other people they ask us where we live, what our families are like, and perhaps what our interests are, and then they ask, "What do you do?" In the existential sense, we are all defined by our choices and our actions. It is not necessary for wealthy individuals to have salaried positions but it is essential for them to have something to do.

In New York one member of a wealthy family works full time giving away the family money through the family foundation. As the executive director of the foundation he is paid one dollar a year! Yet he works as hard as any other executive and those efforts give his life meaning.

This man's lifestyle is in sharp contrast to that of an heiress who has never worked or contributed to the community in any way. As the beneficiary of a very generous trust, she has made a career of sculpting herself, with one facelift or other type of cosmetic surgery after the other, in a never-ending quest for perfection. Clearly she has problems with self-esteem and with accepting herself. In moments of candor she muses about how her life seems to have slipped away.

Both of these individuals have trusts as well as independent funds to which they have direct access. They share the same ethnic heritage. Their family backgrounds are similar: their grandfathers generated vast wealth early in the century and their fathers compounded it. So why are their lives so different? The answer is embedded in their respective family histories, which themselves are a study in contrasts.

The woman—we will call her Judith—was raised by parents whose stated goal in life was to see that none of their children ever wanted for anything. Judith and her brothers and sister were told that they would always be taken care of and never had to worry about a thing. The children got the message their parents sent: they have never worried for a thing that money can buy.

The family in which the man—we will call him Mark—grew up is at the other end of the spectrum. Mark's parents were very serious about preventing their substantial wealth from negatively affecting their children. They treated education about money in much the same way many parents treat sex education—that is, they told their children as much as they needed to know when they wanted to know it. They recognized that children should have what they need and not always what they want. This family is full of stories of how the parents made it clear that just because people have resources does not mean that they get everything they want.

Education for Fiscal Responsibility

A child's education about money begins early. Teaching children about money is similar to teaching them to be responsible for themselves. When children are small, parents must set a well-defined frame of reference and establish boundaries so that they are safe and secure. As they grow and explore the world, the boundaries and responsibilities expand, until as young adults and then as adults they control their own frames of reference.

Mark's parents started doing this early. Even when very young, Mark and his siblings had to set aside a portion of the money they received for charity. Each child's donation was kept separately. Annually each would decide how to disburse it. As the children reached their early teens, the family selected a community service project every year and all the family members worked on it.

When they reached their teens, Mark and his siblings were given a checkbook, a credit card, and a budget determined by their school needs and other activities. Based on that budget, Mark was given an appropriate monthly amount. His credit card bill had to be paid and he had to balance his checkbook. When he went to college Mark was given a single check to cover tuition, housing, and all anticipated expenses for the year. Because his parents had taught individual responsibility from an early age, he was ready to take charge of his own financial affairs and to live with the consequences of his own actions.

When the children reached fifteen, Mark's parents informed them of the existence of a trust fund. The initial description was intentionally vague. The parents emphasized that it was there for college expenses, special experiences, and any emergency that might arise. They emphasized that each child had to make plans for his or her own career and be able to take care of himself or herself.

They told them that each would have control of the funds in the trust when he or she reached age thirty. As the children became comfortable with the information, the parents began to educate them about the importance of keeping the family financial information confidential. "We only talk about these matters with other family members or special advisors," they explained.

When he was twenty, Mark asked his father how much was in the trust. His father replied, "Is it important for you to know that now? Please think about that overnight and give me your answer." The next day Mark came back and asked his father to tell him if the amount was a little or a lot. This time the answer came, "It is substantial." At age twenty-five, in his first year of graduate school, Mark asked for the exact figure. He was surprised but not overwhelmed when he learned that the trust contained millions. Unlike the young man described earlier in this chapter, he had no desire to buy a personal Lear jet. He said, "Well, I guess I will have to get ready to take charge of that when I am thirty." The years of thoughtful effort by his parents had paid off!

Mark's story is one of learning responsibility for self. It is a story of parents who understand what they have to do and do it well. Mark's parents were clear about their values and went to great lengths to instill them in their children.

Unlike Mark, Judith is a sad case. Indeed, she is not the one to blame, she is simply playing out a script written by her parents. Although she has independent funds, she never will have control of the trust that provides her with all her money. At age sixty-two she still has to go to the trustee and make special application for funds. In effect, the trust mechanism keeps her in an adolescent position. Like a child, she can never make her own decisions.

A Case History

In the mid-1980s a family business consultant was working with a large family with extensive real estate holdings. The nine children in the third generation ranged in age from twenty-four to thirty-nine. Their ownership in the holdings was through a series of trusts that was controlled by their parents. The family had a long history of communication about the holdings, the trusts, and their operation. Each of the trusts contained real estate holdings ranging in value from $25 million to $40 million. The second-generation members had wisely distributed enough money to each beneficiary to pay individual taxes and a little more. Then in a family meeting one of the third generation said, "I've been told I'm wealthy all of my life. So where's the beef?"

Because of the nonliquid nature of the real estate business it made sense to keep the holdings intact as a unified asset base but it did not make sense for the third generation to have no autonomy over some portion of the assets they shared. It was proposed that there be created an MIM, short for money for independent management. After extensive discussion with the members of the older and younger generations, the decision was made to disburse $1 million after-tax dollars to each child.

At first there was concern, consternation, and genuine anxiety. With great financial acumen, the family initiated a yearlong process to educate the younger generation about what to do with their money, how to select financial advisors, how to interpret the various forms of financial and investment instruments, and other related matters. They were also taught in detail about the transaction that generated the $9 million thus distributed: a property was sold, the taxes paid, and the money distributed.

As this book is written, it is seven years since the transaction took place and we can fully evaluate its consequences. Some of the children put the money into homes. One bought a restaurant to add to others he already owned and operated. Five formed an investment pool that they named "Gee Tree Investments." It has about $2 million in holdings with different individuals owning different portions. One purchased a block of land for development. These eight proved to be very responsible with their money.

One of the nine began to spend wildly, exceeding her budget and putting her MIM at risk. She met with a consultant to discuss her spending patterns and decided that even though she was thirty-four and a single mother she was not prepared to manage her own financial affairs. She is now back in the former arrangement where her trustee handles her financial affairs.

Partly because of the training they received and partly because of the family orientation, most have tended to invest conservatively. All nine say that the MIM was the single most important step taken to help them mature and be responsible for themselves. The trusts had been operated as if this group of nine were destined to be irresponsible spendthrifts. The MIM was a mechanism that kept the bulk of the asset base intact while encouraging independence, autonomy, and a sense of self-worth and self-esteem.

The principles behind the MIM for young heirs are straightforward:

1. Educate young people to be responsible for themselves.

2. Put a substantial amount of money into their hands and let them manage it. (Define what is meant by substantial on the basis of the family's net worth.)

3. Monitor progress and encourage open discussion in the family about how individuals are managing their funds. In effect, train the younger generation to become a money management support group.

4. If someone is having difficulty, discuss the matter with that person and suggest other alternatives.

5. Be creative in your solutions rather than locked into an archaic mechanism that keeps individuals in an adolescent posture relative to their holdings.

6. Aim for a well-informed family group that has open communication about all matters; there is no substitute for it.

Summary

In this chapter we looked at some of the ways in which family business advisors can assist families in the psychological and personal challenges of growing up wealthy. As advisors work with a family, they will stumble upon its sensitivities, vulnerabilities, and avoidance in dealing with money issues. Advisors themselves have to face these personal issues in order to help open up the family to dealing with financial and related issues.

Summary

Chapter Ten

Planning the Family Estate

Whether you are an attorney experienced in the technical aspects of trusts, estates, and wills or a professional advisor with little experience in such intricacies, the presence—or the lack—of an estate plan is bound to affect the work you do for your family business clients. In addition, your work may have an impact on the estate plan. For instance, a banker primarily concerned with making commercial loans to a family business has concerns about who will control the company after the present owner dies and about the future company's ability to pay back such loans. An insurance agent needs to understand the objectives and provisions of estate documents in order to ensure that policies owned by trusts will provide income tax free proceeds to beneficiaries.

What Is Estate Planning?

Estate planning involves the creation of documents that direct the transfer of property from the owner to others (family members, charitable organizations) in the most tax-efficient fashion. When the property is a family business and cash is needed to cover estate taxes, the task is far more complex, both technically and psychologically. Professional advisors need to understand the emotional issues family business clients will ultimately need to confront in estate planning. A succession plan, in which an owner arranges for the next generation of ownership and management of the company, is an important part of a family business owner's estate plan. (See Chapter Eight for a discussion of succession.)

Owners are often ambivalent about the estate planning process and uncertain about the wisdom of their own decisions. The owner's spouse and children face the prospect of the transfer of property with a mixture of eagerness and fear. They may be uncertain about their ability to manage the business or reluctant to give a sibling lifelong control of the principal family asset. The surviving spouse, who may not have been active in the business, may also have grave concerns about the children's ability to manage the business at a level capable of maintaining current lifestyles. Owners may also avoid estate planning because of fear of confronting their own death or denial of that reality or fear of confronting the death of a parent or spouse. No wonder developing an estate plan can trigger great psychological stress, family dissension, delays in implementation of the plan, and in some cases, frustration of the plan by legal action!

Such negative effects of estate planning can be mitigated if all family members who will be affected have an opportunity to air their concerns and opinions about the plan's goals and objectives. The greater the communication before an estate plan is created, the less likely the family is to be mired in misunderstandings, conflict, and pain later on. Thus one objective of estate planners and other family business advisors is to encourage business owners to formulate and articulate their key estate planning goals. These goals are often the following:

- Reducing future estate taxes by putting assets in trusts or gifting assets to children
- Having the children guarantee their parents an acceptable living standard
- Monitoring the effectiveness and strength of the business to provide for future growth and the parents' needs

Another critical objective is to give heirs an opportunity to understand these goals and to challenge aspects that are not consistent with their wishes.

You don't have to be an estate attorney or a tax expert to raise these issues and to use process consulting tools to help your clients overcome resistance to the process and identify their goals.

Gathering Information

Family advisors can play an important role in the estate planning process. A trusted advisor who has a longstanding relationship with the owners and their families may be influential in prodding them to begin the process. Furthermore, in the course of an advisor's work, information collected about the family business and its members is bound to include some that will be required by an estate planner. It is a good idea to get a client's permission to meet with other advisors they have retained in order to share information and observations about the family and the business.

The information that estate planners need includes a list of current shareholders, officers, and directors and legal documents such as articles of incorporation, bylaws, copies of recent valuations, corporate financial reports, existing wills, voting trust agreements, and partnership agreements if partnerships control some of the shares. You may come across much of this information as you carry out the activities outlined in the earlier chapters of this book. For example, Chapter Four describes how to assess the family and the business. Chapter Five describes how to develop a family mission statement, which is an important document for review in the estate planning process.

Although we suggest throughout this book that advisors consider the family business system as the client, when it comes to estate planning the owner—whose assets are at stake—is the client. However, a conscientious advisor is responsible for telling owners the consequences of their decisions and the extent to which they will affect the interests and security of the spouse, children, and business.

When the estate planning process begins, the first meeting with the family business planner may include both the owner and spouse. In some cases, owners insist on excluding the spouse in order to be free to talk candidly about both the spouse and the children and any pitfalls or problems they envision for the future. It is the advisor's obligation to encourage owners to advise their spouses and other family members fully about their intentions.

When clients are reluctant to share their thoughts and plans, it may be helpful to explore their concerns and objectives for significant others. For example, if an owner claims, "The information is just too complex for my wife to understand," you may answer that it is important for her to meet with someone who can explain it so she will have confidence in the people designated to execute the plan and will know who to turn to when it becomes effective. To owners who wish the information to remain private, you can explore the impact this would have on heirs who would not have the opportunity to talk about their concerns or questions with the person leaving the money or the business to them.

If clients refuse to bring others into the discussions, always leave the door open to do so later on and document as well as possible the owner's thinking so that it is available in the future. Finally, regularly look for opportunities to raise the issue again.

Often family traditions have excluded the consideration of women from active roles in business leadership. Advisors may find that the owners' assumptions about the capabilities of their daughters, nieces, or granddaughters are erroneous. For instance, they may assume that these women do not have the interest in or capability to serve on the board or in management positions even when they have significant business experience and credentials. Such assumptions lead to exclusions, even requests to relinquish stock when "pruning" family stock ownership. The best interests of the business and family may be served by considering all potential leaders and owners.

During the first meeting, the advisor should try to understand the owner's perspective on the business and the family. (Chapter

Two discusses this issue in more detail.) The owner should describe the history of the business—how it started, how it grew, what its current strengths and weaknesses are, who contributes to it and what they contribute, and what the owner's expectations for the future are. Discussions should begin by emphasizing continuation of the business with the current owner in charge. The advisor should learn about any plans to sell the business, take it public, or change its nature in some form.

The next step is to inquire about the current status of management. Who is on the management team? What are their roles? Who serves on the board of directors, if there is one, and who are the officers? How effectively does the owner feel they function? What role, if any, does the owner's spouse play in the business? Whether or not the spouse is actively involved in the business, does he or she enhance or detract from business and family harmony? Are other family members involved at the senior level? What is the owner's perception of the abilities, interests, and business experience of each child and each son-in-law or daughter-in-law? Are any capable of moving into senior management? Does the owner expect any of those employed at the business to continue working there?

This exercise generally leads to one of two paths. If the owner's spouse and children appear interested and capable of continuing to work in the business, the estate plan will focus on protecting the business from transfer taxes and creating control mechanisms such as trusts that will own company stock for successors. In contrast, if the family seems neither interested in nor capable of running the business, the plan will focus on methods for disposing of the business during the current owner's lifetime or after death.

The advisor's job at this stage is not to resolve any family problems but to identify the emotional and technical issues the estate planner will need to factor into an estate plan process. If the advisor can't build consensus among the family around the estate plan, it may be a good idea to bring in a therapist or specialist in family dynamics and systems. However, even this should not impede the estate plan. The owner should still be prodded to move ahead with the development of goals that will form the basis for the drafting of documents. If you are an estate planner or an attorney, you will prepare these documents. If not, you should seek proper counsel to do so. Whatever role you play, the first step after all the necessary information is in hand is to sort through general planning principles and objectives.

Formulating Objectives

The advisor must begin formulating planning objectives by creating a context for the decision-making process. For an attorney or accountant, this process may include an analysis of the transfer taxes that will be imposed on the property if it is transferred during the owner's lifetime or after death. If taxes will be deferred by taking advantage of the unlimited marital deduction, the advisor should help the owner decide the forms in which income will be distributed to the spouse and the kinds of control that the spouse, trustees, and investment advisors of the trust might have. The advisor should also walk the client through the postdeath administration process: the short-term role of executor, interim director, and officer; deadlines for payment of taxes; the audit process. An estate plan describes what will happen in the long term; in the short term, an executor may control the company and vote shares. If the owner prefers, an investment advisory committee can be formed, consisting of several family members who will have the power to vote the stock.

The advisor should help the owner focus on a number of key business issues, including retention of control, timing and mechanics of a shift in control to others, present and future capacity of the company to generate income, income needs of the spouse and children, and the tax and nontax advantages of equity transfers. Many owners wish to maintain control but may be willing to transfer substantial portions of the business equity to their children either currently or in the future.

There are other issues that advisors should help owners think through. Should they leave different assets to different beneficiary groups (for example, company voting shares to children active in the business and real estate to inactive children)? What happens if a member of one beneficiary group dies before the owner? Would the deceased beneficiary's children take the same type of property? The older generation must first decide what they want the estate plan to accomplish by considering not only the tax issues but such personal issues as the effect of wealth on descendants, the level of communications between generations about the estate plan, and the role of charity in the plan. One family business consultant has said, "A thoughtless will can cause generations of distress and chaos. It is imperative that the person making the will first clarify what he or she wants to do with with their assets. If you don't have that clarity at the outset, then taxes are going to drive the process."

Once you have helped clarify the client's objectives you (or the estate planning practitioner) will help translate them into appropriate action, such as preparing leveraged gifting devices or testamentary arrangements or purchasing hedging investments such as insurance.

Discussing Tentative Plans

The spouse should be fully involved at this stage. If the client intends to set aside property in trust for the spouse subject to some limitations and restrictions, the spouse must understand that. Involving the spouse also gives the owner the opportunity to rearticulate the planning objectives and test them against the spouse's desires. Such discussion often leads the owner to modify the estate plan. The process of reviewing objectives (which is much like reviewing assumptions, discussed in Chapter Six) is crucial for ensuring that the plan will be administered without dissension after the owner's death. Advisors can help owners recognize the hidden fears or concerns that are roadblocks to resolution of the issues and persuade them that open, healthy dialogue about the plan and its ramifications for stakeholders is critical.

The children's understanding and embracing of the plan is equally important. It may be possible for the owner to satisfy everyone's objectives if both parents and children understand one another's intentions and perspectives from the outset. Advisors may help foster communication about sensitive issues by first interviewing family members individually and gaining an understanding of their feelings, assumptions, and concerns about the estate planning process.

The owner would be wise to call a family meeting (see Chapter Five) to present the initial drafts of estate planning documents and to discuss the implications. Wealthy families often have a number of irrevocable trusts put in place by a previous generation that they fold into the new planning documents. The family meeting is a good time to present the children with an overview of the historical documents. Everyone may know that Grandfather created some irrevocable trusts but what do they say and what do they mean? This discussion will emphasize openness and information sharing and explain how Grandfather's trust will become part of the planning decisions being made today.

Such sessions can be both informative and conciliatory. The children often view the process as an active affirmation of their maturity and responsibility. If the draft documents establish one child rather than others to act as a fiduciary or to run the business, it is often best to put the issues on the table as early as possible in the process and to provide a reasonable explanation for the decisions. This minimizes later misunderstandings or bad feelings.

In some cases, the owner's objectives may be at loggerheads with those of the children, especially when it comes to issues such as sharing control of the business during the owner's lifetime. Advisors may be able to offer alternatives and compromises that both parties will find acceptable. Sometimes the process may be too divisive and the children will not be persuaded to embrace the owner's plans. In such cases, the owner must ultimately make a decision and the planner must implement that decision in the planning documents. Even so, when the owner takes the time to explain carefully considered decisions and to listen to feedback, most children ultimately understand that it's not their money and that they ought to respect their father's decision, not fight it.

Some children take a "hands-off" approach and decline to offer any reactions or responses to the estate plan. In some cases, solicitation for feedback meets with a steely silence. Something about the plan may irritate them but they want to avoid confrontation. They feel it is their parents' money that is in question and their parents can do whatever they want to with it, even though they themselves consider the plan to be poor. In other cases, the children adore their parents and believe that any plan they make must be terrific. Then there are the children of autocratic parents. These children never question anything their parents have done—doing so simply is not part of the family dynamic.

The advisor and the parents may have to help children like these break through their reserve by posing very specific questions as they describe each provision. For instance, an advisor may say, "We're thinking of designating Bill to vote the shares because he'll be running the business while Sharleen and Dan both live far away and won't be active in the business. But there may be issues Sharleen and Dan may want to vote on, for instance, if Bill wants to sell the business. What do you all think?" In this way the advisor may help the children identify issues that are of importance to them.

Some owners are reluctant to discuss their plans with their children. One family business owner who had four very competent children ranging in age up to forty didn't want them to know anything about the estate plan; the estate planner tried in vain to convince the owner to inform them. Advisors may not always succeed, but they should try to encourage owners to share information that will affect the children, especially if they have been chosen for roles of responsibility.

The family meeting is also a good place to broach the subject of inheriting wealth and how heirs should be educated to be responsible and competent in their handling of money. (This subject is detailed in Chapter Nine.)

After the family meeting, the advisor and parents may reconvene to discuss the plan and make modifications that incorporate the children's objectives. Most families want to accommodate the wishes of their children. To the extent that doing so is possible the estate plan will be immeasurably strengthened and the family will run far less risk of future division.

There may be issues the parents are not willing to compromise on. Even so, the exercise of sharing information is bound to be useful. The ultimate success of the plan will be enhanced if the children have a real opportunity to comment on the decisions and express their views. In most cases, the very act of holding a family meeting suggests that the children are the beneficiaries and are cared for.

When the final set of documents and decisions are made, parents should discuss them with the children. The parents may wish to explain why any clearly expressed objectives of the children are not satisfied. Parents should sign the new documents even if the decisions are divisive because they reflect some hard decisions. They may then secure more sophisticated consulting services to help resolve any serious tensions that may have been exposed in the planning process.

Breaking Through Procrastination

Advisors frequently act as catalysts. Each step of the decision-making process may create delays, uncertainties, and a desire on the client's part to put the issue off to another day. People tend to freeze up if disagreements surface during the planning process. They fear they may make a bad decision and this causes them to proceed slowly if at all. As a result, preexisting documents, which may be outdated and inconsistent with their current objectives, may remain in place and govern the disposition of the business at the owner's death. Worse, there may be no preexisting documents. If the owner dies intestate (without a legal will), all assets will be held up in probate court, which may not distribute assets as the owner would have liked. Probate courts make no effort to minimize estate taxes so the bill will be likely to erode an unnecessarily large portion of the estate.

Advisors should emphasize that planning is an ongoing process. No estate plan can accommodate all the competing needs and interests. No plan is perfect. The documents should, however, reflect the best judgments that can be made today with the understanding that irresolvable issues will be addressed again at some future point. Advisors can be very useful simply by pushing and nagging clients toward completion of a plan, even if both client and advisor acknowledge that it is imperfect and will have to be revised in the future. Procrastination often assumes one of three forms.

Complete paralysis. Family business owners who realize they're "surrounded" are so overwhelmed by warring family factions that they choose to do nothing. They won't even talk to an estate planning practitioner.

Often advisors other than lawyers or other estate planning practitioners can be useful. Insurance agents, lenders, accountants, and bankers who work with the owners regularly are all in a position to tell such clients they need to develop a plan that will protect the family and business after the owners die.

Feeling stuck at square one. Some owners begin to talk to existing advisors about issues raised by the prospect of estate planning. Each question presents a difficult decision so the owners become "stuck" at this preplanning stage and choose to worry about inventory or cash flow instead of estate planning. Advisors can tug hard to get all or part of relevant documents drafted in the form of a trust or will that reflects the owners' objectives.

Fear of signing on the dotted line. Many clients make a good start: they find a professional, share all necessary information, and delineate their objectives. But when the professional returns with all the carefully drafted documents, they say, "Let me sit on this. I'll call you after I've thought about it," and the professional waits and waits. Some owners are superstitious, believing that if they sign the documents, they'll instantly die. Others feel insecure about the decisions they've come to. Sometimes just one little unresolved point stymies the entire process. One owner could not decide whether to give 25 percent or 30 percent of his money to charity in the unlikely event that his entire family were to die. This provision impeded execution of the entire document.

Advisors should continuously emphasize the need to take action: make preliminary decisions, get them onto paper, and execute those documents. One of the authors of this book worked with a client for eighteen months to get a comprehensive plan adopted. It was signed on September 28, 1993, and the eighty-year-old patriarch died October 8, 1993. Had the documents not been signed, it would have put the large business into chaos. The clear message is this: get something done—you never know what is coming.

A trusted friend is often a good influence to get past procrastination or dreadful stories that owners may have heard about loss of control, excessive taxes, years in probate court, or conflict and will contests because the deceased had failed to indicate personal preferences.

Continuing the Planning Process

Once the initial plan is completed the documents should be drawn up and signed. At this stage, the family business advisor should see that two things are accomplished. First, the principles that underlie the documents should be rearticulated and reemphasized. Clients should clearly understand what the documents say with respect to the retention and disposition of the business and the retention and ultimate transfer of control and the enjoyment of income. They should appreciate how their children will share in the growth and control of the business when they pass from the scene. Second, advisors should emphasize that the plan is not cast in stone and will require change from time to time, as estate tax laws, the business, and the family's needs and interests change.

Family members, whether satisfied with the decisions or not, will at least know the framework for the disposition of the family wealth and understand the role each member will be expected to play. Their peace of mind will erode, however, if there is constant fine-tuning of the documents without the participation of beneficiaries. Children are likely to become uneasy about the process if their parents are constantly changing their minds and perhaps the agreed-on rules of disposition. They may feel disenfranchised and uninformed. They will feel uneasy if subsequent decisions are made without the sort of exchanges that characterized the earlier planning process.

If a client insists on updating documents consistently, such changes should be discussed with the children, perhaps during the annual family meetings. Family meetings also offer children an opportunity to revisit issues previously discussed that may have become less difficult with time. A child may have resigned from the company, the company may be generating substantially more or less income, or the business outlook may be significantly different. The fact that the owners sought the counsel of the children earlier and are doing so again allows for open and useful discussion in a non-hostile setting and permits the plan to continue to evolve with greater continuity and stability.

Summary

The process described in this chapter is not always perfect, but it is necessary and generally leads to some peace of mind for the family business client. There is no easy formula for the estate planning process. Each family, business, and individual personality is different. Family business advisors must rely on their own experience to suggest solutions and formats for the planning process. Sharing information and creating a forum for discussion about it is often the most useful. Even complex estate plans can be successfully implemented if they are presented openly and candidly with family members on an ongoing basis.

Chapter Eleven

Conclusion: Heeding the Call for Professionalism

We have come to the end of our journey. We hope this book has succeeded in its attempt to build on your professional experience in order to offer you insights, perspectives, models, and tools that will expand and change your view of the family business and your options for your practice. As we have said many times, it is not our intention to disrupt or disparage advisors' practice of their disciplines. Rather, we have tried to identify common themes and difficulties that arise in any professional discipline when it comes to working with family businesses and to provide perspectives and tools that lead to helpful intervention.

What should you do now? First, we hope you will see the families you work with in a different light. By adopting the family systems perspective, you may see the different contexts and deeper issues that lie behind the individual requests your clients make of you. This should lead you to ask some different questions of them and to move in new directions.

Second, we hope you will involve more people in your work. You may want to include more family members in your consultations or suggest a family gathering. The family systems perspective will help you understand why some families you work with seem to ignore or neglect their best interests or resist good advice. You can help them get around resistance by helping them see the obstacles they have put in their own ways. The family systems perspective should enable you to see the problems more clearly and accomplish your work more effectively.

Finally, we also believe that your practice will benefit if you move out of the expert role at times and use some of the tools of process consulting. We do not recommend that you make a head-long plunge into this new arena but rather that you adopt some of the tools and techniques we have described as you come upon appropriate situations. We suggest that you experiment slowly and become comfortable with such techniques as setting up a family retreat or helping a family create more effective governance structures.

The following list summarizes the assumptions we have set forth in this book:

- It is important to understand the family business as a complex system composed of a series of interdependent subsystems.

- A developmental perspective (of the individual, the family, and the business) is useful in understanding the challenges a family business faces.

- Communication through the whole system is critical to success for advisors of all kinds.

- The perspectives of all stakeholders are legitimate in the problem-solving process.

- A framework for communication and clear organizational structures, policies, and appropriate boundaries must be developed.

- Because a range of perspectives and skills are needed to serve family businesses effectively, advisors need to broaden their own capabilities and to collaborate with other professionals who can complement them.

Family businesses are complex organizations that challenge some of the conventional training and wisdom of our professions. Serious consideration of the unique processes, dynamics, and issues they face, however, is a recent phenomenon. It is therefore important that all the professionals serving family businesses engage in an ongoing dialogue.

We hope that our efforts to share the assumptions underlying our own work with family businesses has helped to begin this dialogue. The dialogue process requires that we all bring our own assumptions to the fore and explore them. We hope that this book has helped you examine your assumptions about working with family businesses as well as those that we presented. Undoubtedly we challenged some of your assumptions. Our goal was not to convert you to our perspective but to expose you to the range of roles advisors can play, the perspectives they can take, the tools they can use, and the resources they can deploy in assisting family businesses.

We hope you will continue the dialogue process by sharing your reactions and observations with us. Ultimately, we all must develop shared assumptions about our work with family business clients if we wish to enhance our objectivity, skills, and resourcefulness.

We close by emphasizing a final intention of this book: to help family businesses thrive as effective businesses and as nurturing environments for their members. Professional advisors often have unique and powerful insights into the most important family activities. They may have a powerful impact on the family or unnecessarily limit themselves and therefore miss the opportunity to offer something the family needs not just to overcome a crisis but to move to a higher level. In this book we have invited you to grow, to learn, and to develop as a professional family business advisor.

Resources

Here we describe some key works that expand on the ideas we presented in this book.

Addiction Research Foundation. (1994). *Dealing with substance abuse in small businesses: Results of a qualitative study.* Toronto: Addiction Research Foundation.

This helpful guide explains how to perceive and act on issues that are caused by substance abuse in organizations.

Aronoff, C., and Ward, J. (eds.). (1991). *Family business sourcebook.* Detroit: Omnigraphics.

This anthology of important articles published for professionals on the issues and concerns of family business includes nearly one hundred selections from all media sources. It contains many classic articles offering information on all aspects of family business consultation.

Bork, D. (1993). *Family business, risky business.* Aspen, Colo.: Aspen Family Business Group.

This book offers comprehensive coverage of family systems dynamics in relation to family businesses. It includes a representative case history of the different dilemmas and choices faced by family businesses. It offers excellent coverage of substance abuse as an issue in family business.

Brown, F. H. (ed.). (1991). *Reweaving the family tapestry.* New York: Norton.

This book of readings about multigenerational family systems perspectives describes specific tools, including creating a family genogram. It is a good next step after the present book for professionals who want to learn more about working with multigenerational family systems. Some selections on family business are included.

Cohn, M. (1994). *Passing the torch: Succession, retirement, and estate planning in family-owned businesses.* **(2nd ed.) New York: McGraw-Hill.**

This is a family systems-informed account of the key issues in estate and succession planning. It offers detailed explanations of the more important activities and explains how to balance the different needs of different subsystems.

Ibrahim, A. B., and Ellis, W. H. (1994). *Family business management: Concepts and practices.* **Dubuque, Iowa: Kendall/Hunt.**

This basic textbook for family business courses presents the concepts of business, financial, family, management, and personal development and the major theories and models of family business.

Jaffe, D. (1990). *Working with the ones you love: Strategies for a successful family business.* **Emeryville, Calif.: Conari Press.**

This step-by-step how-to book guides family businesses and advisors as they navigate the predictable problems that family businesses face. It describes many exercises and assessment tools. It offers instructions for leading family retreats and information on building collaboration in the family and in the business.

Poza, E. J. (1989). *Smart growth: Critical choices for business growth and prosperity.* **San Francisco: Jossey-Bass.**

This is a comprehensive guide to navigating the different stages of small and medium-size business growth and development, including business, strategy, and management issues. An excellent guide to business development.

Schein, E. (1987). *Process consultation,* **Vol. 2. Reading, Mass.: Addison Wesley.**

This basic introduction to process consultation by MIT professor and consultant Schein offers guidelines for its practice and ground rules for its use. A basic introduction to skills.

Ward, J. (1991). *Creating effective boards for private enterprises: Meeting the challenges of continuity and competition.* San Francisco: Jossey-Bass.

This book offers a practical explanation of why outsiders need to be involved in a family business board, how to organize them, how to balance different stakeholder groups, and how to use the board as a vehicle for business development. The book is full of practical advice and case histories.

Index

A

Abandonment, 65–66
Accountability, 103, 146; of family versus other employees, 153–154
Accountants, 6, 163, 172
Activities, family, 64–65
Addiction. *See* Substance abuse
Addiction Research Foundation, 217
Adult development, 45–47
Advisors, 1; dialogue among, 214–215; involvement style of, 19–24; issues faced by, 3–4, 6; role of, in conflict situations, 111; role of, in estate planning, 199, 201–205, 208–210; role of, in family business consulting, 5–7, 8–9, 19–24, 30–31, 158; role of, in family work session, 92–93; role of, in succession, 163–164, 174, 178–179; role of, in wealth management, 183–184, 197; styles of, 10–11; styles of, choosing among, 19–24; for substance abuse interventions, 132; types of, 6. *See also* Collaboration among advisors; Expert advisors; Family systems–informed experts; Process consultants
Advisory boards, 141, 147
Agendas: for family work session, 95, 96–101; multiple, 90; sample, 96–101
Alcoholics Anonymous (AA), 134, 135
Alcoholism. *See* Substance abuse
American Bar Association (ABA), 13
Anasazi Indians, 187–189
Aronoff, C., 217
Assessment: of business's financial health, 77–81; of compensation policies, 77–76; of competency, 73–74; data gathered in, 72–83; of employment policies, 74, 76; formal process of, 69–70; of legal documents, 76–77; of market potential, 81–82; of motivation, 73–74; of physical assets, 80–81; purposes of, 70–72; reporting on, to family, 83–84; for succession planning, 174. *See also* Data collection
Assets: protection from deteriorating, 176; sale of, 178–180
Assumptions, 99, 119–120

B

Bankers, 6, 163; cost of, 180; and estate planning, 199
Beneficiaries, 205
Bingham family, 5
Blended family, 56
Boards of directors, 148–150, 158. *See also* Family boards
Boards. *See* Advisory boards; Boards of directors; Family boards
Boundaries: between advisor and family business, 111; between business and family, 16–17, 23, 140, 149–150, 173–174; business structures for managing, 139–150; and confidentiality, 190; healthy family, 44, 66; organizational policies for managing, 150–158; and redefining relationships, 157–158; and succession planning, 173–174. *See also* Business structures; Policy making
Brainstorming, 114–115
Brown, F. H., 43, 217–218

HENRY HARDER